MW01515387

"Today's highly competitive and embattled job market is difficult enough without the proper tools to navigate it. In *How to Get and Keep a Job*, Donna Watson, PhD, offers such a tool via sensible, easy-to-follow guidelines—from the job hunt to interviewing, from first impressions to creative communication skills, from time management to making powerful presentations—that take the candidate through the process and into professional success once on the job."

—Kathleen Samuelson
Publications Director, CBA
CBA Retailers+Resources Magazine

"Every student needs to read this book. It provides the necessary career skills to launch them into their profession."

—William P. Goad, Jr, EdD
Professor of Business
Executive Vice President
Oklahoma Christian University

"*How to Get and Keep a Job* is a valuable source for anyone seeking employment."

—Michael J. O'Keefe, MFA
Professor, Art+Design
Oklahoma Christian University

"Gardner & Associates works with a range of not for profit organizations (NPOs). In sharing the draft model of *How to Get and Keep a Job*, our client responses have been highly positive. NPOs working with minority, work force or youth constituencies indicated that they welcome Dr. Watson's practical, simple approach to a real world challenge. They see this as a reasonable and affordable curriculum for their constituents- those with the greatest need and most to gain."

—Walt Eilers
Gardner & Associates
479.283.2784 mobile
www.whygardner.com
Growing philanthropy

"If this is not the most needed book in the country, I don't know what it would be."

—Dr. Richard Tate
Founder & Chairman of the Board
Tate Publishing Inc

"Read it! Do it!"

—Monte E. Farrar
HR Training Manager
Express Employment Professionals

"With unemployment at an all-time high, every job seeker needs an edge. This book gives you the tools to land the job...and hold on to it."

—Shay Lastra
Owner
Nsite Language Services

How To
Get
And
Keep
a Job

How To Get And Keep a Job

Donna S. Watson, PhD

TATE PUBLISHING & *Enterprises*

How to Get and Keep a Job
Copyright © 2011 by Donna S. Watson, PhD. All rights reserved.

No part of this publication may be reproduced, stored in a retrieval system or transmitted in any way by any means, electronic, mechanical, photocopy, recording or otherwise without the prior permission of the author except as provided by USA copyright law.

All scripture quotations, unless otherwise indicated, are taken from the *Holy Bible, New International Version*®. niv®. Copyright © 1973, 1978, 1984 by International Bible Society. Used by permission of Zondervan. All rights reserved.

Scripture quotations marked (kjv) are taken from the *Holy Bible, King James Version*, Cambridge, 1769. Used by permission. All rights reserved.

The opinions expressed by the author are not necessarily those of Tate Publishing, LLC.

Published by Tate Publishing & Enterprises, LLC
127 E. Trade Center Terrace | Mustang, Oklahoma 73064 USA
1.888.361.9473 | www.tatepublishing.com

Tate Publishing is committed to excellence in the publishing industry. The company reflects the philosophy established by the founders, based on Psalm 68:11,
"The Lord gave the word and great was the company of those who published it."

Book design copyright © 2011 by Tate Publishing, LLC. All rights reserved.
Cover design by Blake Brasor
Interior design by Lindsay B. Behrens

Published in the United States of America

ISBN: 978-1-61777-405-8
1. Business & Economics / Careers / Job Hunting
2. Business & Economics / Careers / Resumes
11.08.01

DEDICATION

This book is dedicated to my fantastic husband, without whom I would only be half a person. He completes my life in a way that no other could and believes in me even when I lose belief in myself.

Thank you, Robert, for picking up where my wonderful parents left off and never losing faith in me and in who I can become. I will love you forever.

A SPECIAL NOTE OF THANKS

There are so many who have helped, encouraged, and believed in me on this journey that it is hard to list them by name for fear of leaving someone out.

Michael O'Keefe, the head of the department at Oklahoma Christian University where I taught this course for most of the last 15 years, was the first to suggest that I put this book together. My husband, always the ready supporter, told me to go for it.

As the book progressed and needed editing, I turned quickly to my editing gurus, Dr. Rita Goad, Lynda Sheehan, and Sue Zurcher. They made me look good, and I am eternally grateful to them for their help. When final proofing time came, they again stepped up to help, along with Beverly Dillow, Barbara Fielder, Connie Mashburn, and of course, my husband. A special thanks to Mel Milligan who helped me visualize the cover design. My utmost gratitude to all of them.

The followers on my blog helpmelord8.blogspot.com got a daily update while I put this book together in a record 26 days. They were my cheering squad, and I love them for it.

And last, but certainly not least, was Dr. Richard Tate who believed that if this were not the most needed book in the country, he didn't know what it would be. He and his team at Tate Publishing made my dream come true and helped me put together a book that can help people who are struggling to make a better life for themselves and their families. Whether they are graduating and looking for jobs, having to revaluate their job opportunities, or adapting to a new way of life that makes job hunting a whole new ballgame, this book can be their guide.

I am, of course, most grateful to my Lord and Savior without whom none of this could have taken place. He is my guide, my strength and my inspiration. May He so bless each of you as you read and work through this material that the very piece that will help you the most becomes quickly apparent to you. Enjoy!

TABLE OF CONTENTS

Section II
How to Keep a Job
What are They Looking For?

Chapter 4: Skill No. 1 - Attitude

Chapter 5: Skill No. 2 – Goal Setting

Chapter 10: Skill No. 7 - Budgeting

Chapter 11: Skill No. 8 - Stress Management

Section III

How to be on the Competitive Edge

Chapter 12: Communication Skills

Chapter 13: How to Make Powerful Presentations

Chapter 14: Let's Go to Work!

Chapter 15: Practice Speech No. 1

Chapter 16: Practice Speech No. 2

Chapter 17: Practice Speech No. 3

Chapter 18: Practice Speech No. 4

Epilogue

INTRODUCTION

Why should I buy this book?

Unless you are serious about getting and keeping a job and have the desire to do more with your life than just have a job, like having a career, then don't buy this book. Go buy yourself a chocolate sundae. It will do you more good.

By the way, buy a cheap sundae because that is all you will ever be able to afford. Without getting and keeping a job and turning it into a career, you will never be able to consistently afford Haagen Dazs ice cream.

So, you decide. Are you going to buy this book and take it seriously?

What are we going to do in this book?

1. We are going to have fun, as all of life should be fun.
2. We are going to learn how to believe in ourselves because if you don't believe in you, no one else will either.
3. We are going to gain some useful life skills. As Horace Mann, the father of education said, "If education is to mean anything, it must teach us how to live."

How are we going to do these things?

1. We are going to be honest about ourselves.
2. We are going to practice what we learn.
3. We are going to try again and again and again because perfection is never possible, but excellence is.

Why are we going to do these things?

1. Because the most talented people in the world cannot make a living unless they can "sell" their talents. This means **YOU.**

2. Because getting out of school or going from one job to another requires continuous changes in who you are.

3. Because **you are the best**, and until you believe that and can make others see it as well, you will never progress from a job to a career.

Now you know the "why." Are you ready and willing to do what it takes to make your life everything that you deserve for it to be? Yes? Then let's go!

Section I
How to Get a Job

When you try to do things without

Jesus, you will never totally succeed.

If you try to do things with Jesus,

you will never totally fail.

Dr. Virgil Trout

Notes

CHAPTER 1
Getting the Job You Want

I am not young enough to know everything.

Oscar Wilde

People who are most successful at getting the job that they want treat the process seriously. In other words, they **WORK** at job hunting. Leaning back in your chair with the classified ads over your face and snoozing is not looking for a job. It is a proactive process and not an easy one.

First of all, they know what type of job that they want. Then they begin to organize their approach to job hunting and make a pledge to do something every day toward the successful completion of that goal.

Take Job-Hunting Seriously

Do you know what kind of job you want, or are you just looking for anything, something that sounds fun or looks interesting? There is an old adage that says if you aim at nothing, you'll hit it every time. Does that bring you back to the question? What kind of job do you want?

Any job pays more bills than no job.

Take a little time and sit down with a good cup of coffee or an ice cold glass of water, or whatever you prefer, and make a list:

1. What do you do well?
2. What do you enjoy doing?

3. Do you deal well with people?

4. Do you want an office or a factory job?

5. What type of job does your experience prepare you for?

6. Are you interested in a sales job?

7. Are you willing to stand or sit all day?

8. Are you willing to be confined to an office?

9. Are you willing to travel?

10. Are you willing to work evenings and/or weekends?

11. Do you prefer and/or need a job with a regular paycheck or would you consider a job that pays commission?

12. Would you consider moving to another city?

Look at your answers to these questions. Analyze them, and you will have a pretty good idea of the type of job that you are searching for. Is this your "ideal" job? If the answers to these questions don't fall in line with your ideal job, then begin to analyze what it will take to prepare yourself for that type of job.

If you don't know exactly what your ideal job would be, then look at these questions and move in the direction where you are currently best suited. Sometimes we have to try a variety of positions in order to find the one that really suits us. It is like accidently running into a course in school that you never dreamed that you would like and falling in love with it. Sometimes we have to experiment to discover our true selves.

If you had an opportunity to obtain your ideal job, do you:

1. Have the skills necessary to perform that job?

2. Have the experience needed for it?

3. Have the education that job requires?

4. Have the equivalent skills to replace the educational requirements?

5. Have access to getting the needed skills?

6. Agree with the job level that this type of job would provide?

7. Agree with the salary range that this type of job would provide?

8. Dislike any part of the performance requirements for this job?

Pursue Your New Job in an Organized Manner

Looking for a job is a full-time pursuit. You need to organize your time and, without exception, do something every day that will give you another opportunity to find your ideal job, or at least a job.

What are you willing to commit to doing every day to find a job?

Looking for a job is not a hobby or a vacation. Get serious if you really want to go to work. Do these activities every day:

1. **Read** the classified ads, trade publications, online job ads, business publications and professional magazines.

2. **Check out** companies that you are interested in online and see what kind of requirements they have for their jobs, what jobs are available, and if they prefer to have an application snail-mailed or e-mailed to them. Eighty percent of companies are now using LinkedIn as their primary tool to find employees, so don't forget to check that source as well.

3. **Submit** at least one job application daily. It should always be accompanied with a cover letter and mailed or e-mailed to a specific person in the company. (More about this later.)

4. **Set up** a one-on-one meeting with prospective employers as often as possible. Give yourself a chance to impress them face to face. Don't hold back just in case that perfect job comes through. At this point you are looking for a job, not a career.

5. **Network.** Go to meetings, join organizations, volunteer, talk with friends, and check with the Chamber of Commerce to see if they have a meet-and-greet group. Do not stay at home in your jammies and expect the world to come knocking at your door.

6. **Be creative.** Especially if you are looking for hourly work, check bulletin boards in hardware stores, lumber yards, plumbing shops, glass installers, and auto parts stores. Hourly work is usually available in places like grocery stores, salons, restaurants, and quick stops, too. Don't just check what is there; post an ad for yourself. In recent times, people have even come up with ways to feature themselves and their talents on YouTube and make a connection with the company of their dreams. YouTube is the 2nd largest search engine in the world, so don't let your imagination become limited.

You Need a Resume

What is a resume? Basically it is a tool used for helping you get an interview… not a job. The resume is used to open the door so that you will have an opportunity to express how you will benefit their company and what type of skills you have that will meet their needs. It helps to start the process. It does not end it.

A resume is a tool used for helping you get an interview…not a job.

In many situations in our global society, your resume is the only way you will have to make that first impression. Whether the resume is submitted by snail mail or e-mail, it has to make an instant impression. On average, an employer will spend between 45 seconds and 2 minutes looking at your resume. In other words, it has to make an instant impression, or the time you spent preparing it was a total waste. Do it right because you won't get a second chance.

What Is a Good Resume?

A good resume should be so structured that it will show your job objectives, your employment history, and your educational history in the most meaningful manner for that particular type of job.

There are five basic items that go into a good resume:

1. Name, address, phone number, and e-mail address
2. Career objective
3. Education, including all honors and achievements as well as scholarships
4. Work experience
5. References if requested

You do not put your hobbies in your resume. Neither do you provide information about your marital status or family. In fact, some states forbid asking anything about age, ancestry, national origin, race, or religion, and they do not allow employers to ask for a photo. You also don't need to include your social security number, height, weight, or any remarks about your physical appearance or health.

Before we look at the different types of resumes and begin working on the one best suited for your particular job request at this time, let's look at the Dos and Don'ts of resume writing. If you will follow these suggestions when preparing the resume and recheck them before presenting it, then your chances of having it make a good first impression will be greatly enhanced.

Dos of Good Resume Writing

- Do print your resume on standard-sized, white or ivory paper.

- Do have it professionally prepared. Whether you use Microsoft Word or some other means does not matter, but whatever you do, it must *not* be hand written. Be sure when it is professionally prepared, it is neat, clean, and has plenty of white spaces and margins.

- Do use only standard, conventional English. KISS (Keep It Simple, Sweetie) is always the best policy.

- Do use short paragraphs, i.e. no longer than five lines.

- Do proofread. Proofread. Proofread.

- Do write a specific resume for a specific company.

- Do include your outstanding accomplishments from each previous job.

- Do focus on the job experiences that are most relevant.

- Do list only relevant professional, trade, and civic associations.

- Do be sure that your references have a copy of your resume.

- Do always send a cover letter with your resume.

- Do reread your resume just before an interview. They probably did, too.

Don'ts of Good Resume Writing

- Don't put a date of preparation or submission on your resume.

- Don't give reasons for having left a previous job. It will be better to explain in person if asked.

- Don't state, "References Available on Request." This is an assumption.

- Don't use exact dates. Months and years are sufficient.

- Don't list your elementary, middle, or high school if you are a college graduate.

- Don't list your objectives unless the resume is targeted to that particular job or occupation.

- Don't use professional jargon or buzz words.

- Don't provide salary information. It can be discussed during the interview, or if required, it can be presented in the cover letter.

- Don't make the resume too long. A page or two should generally be sufficient.

- Don't lie.

How Do I Choose a Resume Format?

You choose your resume format depending on what is important about you and the type of experience you have. The old standby, the **Chronological** resume, is good for almost everyone. The employment record is the primary organizing principle for this format. It is particularly effective for people who have clear-cut qualifications and who are continuing and advancing in a specific career direction.

The **Functional** format resume might be the best if you have never had an impressive title. This resume focuses on your key skills, accomplishments, and knowledge and how they relate to the particular job you are applying for. It gives you an opportunity to show how your skills and accomplishments from a previous job will transfer to this new position. You may also provide information about unpaid employment and can give status to additional qualifying experience in your life.

A good resume cannot get you a job, but a bad one can prevent you from getting an interview.

The **Special Skills** resume is designed to provide an opportunity to describe skills that you have mastered.

A good resume cannot get you a job, but a bad one can prevent you from getting an interview. It is very appropriate to specialize your resume for a particular type of job or company. In fact, you should. Be accurate, appropriate, and above all, be honest. Employers know that they are not going to get a perfect employee, but they sincerely appreciate an honest one. There are probably fewer rules for resumes today than there have been for some time. Even though you have an opportunity to be somewhat creative, it is still best to focus on key achievements and a conservative style.

Information Needed For a Resume

1. **Work History:**

    a. Create a work history master list.

        i. List paid and unpaid jobs with beginning and ending dates in chronological order.

  ii. List job titles.

  iii. List companies or organizations by name.

  iv. List location of employment.

2. **Education and Training:**

 a. Create an education and training master list.

  i. List schools attended with dates, degrees, and honors.

  ii. List personal study programs.

  iii. List other credentials and certifications.

3. **Job Objective:**

 a. Clearly state job objective in a minimum of words.

  i. What do you want to do?

  ii. Where do you want to do it?

  iii. When do you want to do it?

  iv. Why do you want to do it?

  v. How do you plan to accomplish your objective?

4. **Skills and Experience:**

 a. Assemble a skills and experience sheet by combining specialized talents and abilities into a one-page description.

5. **Specific Credentials:**

 a. Establish a master list of specific credentials.

  i. Determine their relevance.

  ii. Determine their usefulness.

  iii. Add significant accomplishments.

  iv. Add outstanding natural skills.

  v. Refer to your values, philosophies, and commitments.

  vi. Update for use on appropriate resumes.

How to Put the Resume Together

1. Assemble the five parts of your resume: Work History, Education and Training, Job Objective, Skills and Experience, and Specific Credentials.

2. Present the information on one page if possible. If a second page is necessary, write, "continued" on page one and, "page two" along with your full name on the second page.

Check updated versions of resume writing as trends do change.

3. Present the most important information on the first page, and save your work history and education for page two if two pages are necessary.

4. Do not staple the pages together.

There are several excellent books available to assist in this process. It is always a good idea to check an updated version of resume writing as trends do change. You can find good information not only at bookstores but also online and in public libraries. *What Color Is Your Parachute* is published yearly and is an excellent reference for current trends.

The Cover Letter

A professional presentation traditionally required a cover letter or an application letter. In the day of internet interviews, this is not always possible. However, if you can send an e-mail with your application or can figure out a way to send one to the correct person even though it is not attached to the application, it will definitely make you stand out in the crowd.

The cover letter is a personal piece of communication and is more likely to be passed on to someone who is looking for a worker like you than the resume will. It gives you an opportunity to reveal your personality and professionalism in a practical setting.

The cover letter should include:

    a. Correct name and title of the person conducting interviews.

    b. Not just good, but excellent grammar and spelling. Proofread!

    c. Professionally type your letter. No handwritten letters, please!

    d. Use only a professional approach. Clichés and cute remarks are not professional.

    e. The letter should be one page long with three paragraphs:

        i. State the position you are applying for and how you found out about it.

        ii. Tell how you are suited for this particular position and what talents and/or experiences you have that qualify you.

        iii. Tell the reader that you would like an interview and how they can get in touch with you. (You might even offer to call in a few days to set up the appointment, and do so.)

Cover letters are usually quickly evaluated and, as long as they do not have poor spelling, bad grammar, and poor organization, will lead to a quick look at the enclosed resume. They will be rejected quickly if your abilities do not match those that are required for this position or if you over-emphasize your needs or abilities. Sentences such as, "You need to call me right away, as your company cannot survive much longer without me," or, "I am the best person you will find for this job and certainly deserve to be at the top of your salary range," will destroy an interview opportunity in a nanosecond.

Reference Letters

If you have requested reference letters from a previous employer or from friends and associates, be sure that you have a copy of those letters in your files. You have a right to know what is being said about you, and it is okay to request a copy, so don't hesitate to do so.

If you received a poor recommendation, you may request a better one. You at least have the right to an explanation as to why the recommendation was poor.

Be sure that the people you are using for references are aware that their names have been presented. This way they will not be surprised if they receive a call and, having had a chance to be more prepared, they are more likely to give a much better recommendation. Have their full names (and title, if any), addresses, and phone number with you during the interview in case they are requested.

How to Get the Interview

Yay! You have finally found a job you are interested in. Good for you! The next step: get an interview and seal the job.

Follow requests exactly!

How do you do that? If you are responding to an ad from the paper, one on the Internet, or even a referral from a friend, find out what information the company is requesting. They will probably expect a cover letter, accompanied by a resume. You have the basic information ready for both, so go to work.

Follow their requests exactly. This will assure them of not only your sincerity but also your organizational abilities. Some companies will want you to mail the information, and some will want it e-mailed. If it is e-mailed, be sure that you understand whether they want the material within the e-mail itself or whether they prefer that it be sent through an attachment. Some companies will not accept material that is submitted through an attachment.

Address the cover letter to the person indicated in the ad and be very careful to spell the name correctly. If they are local or if you can find the information on the web, you may want to verify that this is the correct spelling of their name and that their title is the same as the one listed in the ad.

Several days after your information is submitted, it is permissible and preferable to call the company and ask if they received your information. (Remember the post office is much slower than the web, so don't rush it.) If it has been received, you should ask if they need any additional information and take this opportunity to once again express your interest in their job. At this time you can tactfully request an interview so that you may learn more about the position and share your qualifications in person. In addition, if you can do any networking with regard to this particular job, then do so.

When you have an interview scheduled, ask for permission to pick up a job description (if they are local) or that one be sent to you (if you must travel for the interview). This will give you a better opportunity to prepare yourself for questions that might be asked and how your qualifications will provide what is needed to fulfill their position.

It is time to research. Never walk into a company for an interview without knowing as much as you can about who they are and what they do. Can you imagine what an interviewer would do if you walked in and said, "By the way, what does this company do?"

This material can come from several sources:

    a. Ask for an annual report.

    b. Check the Internet for a website.

    c. Check your local library.

    d. Check with the Chamber of Commerce.

    e. Check with the Better Business Bureau.

    f. Pick up any brochures they have in their offices.

    g. Ask questions of anyone you might know who deals with them or is associated in any way.

Whatever it takes, find out who they are, what they do, and how they do it.

If you found out about this job opening through an individual, call the company, find out the name of the interviewer (be sure you have their name correct), and ask to speak with them. Tell them how you found out about the job, share your qualifications, and request an interview. If they are interested, they will let you know the procedure to follow in order to get an appointment. Follow it exactly.

In your cover letter to this company, be sure that you remind them that they requested your resume and that you are looking forward to hearing from them.

If the job is not available at the moment but will be upcoming in the near future, then you can still submit a cover letter and resume and refer to your interest in the future position. Check back closer to the date of the opening and see if they have any idea of when they will begin interviews.

The Dos of a Good Interview

1. **Do be on time.** Allow extra time for traffic, parking, getting lost, etc. Remember, if it can happen, it will.

2. **Do dress appropriately.** See the section for professional dress in Chapter 3 of this book and take it very seriously.

3. **Do speak clearly and distinctly.** Not everyone hears as well as you, so please be aware and respectful of their needs.

4. **Do offer a firm handshake and good eye contact**. Remember, you only get one chance to make a good first impression. Read Chapter 3 carefully and more than once, just in case you missed something.

5. **Do be organized.** You should have an extra copy or two or your resume with you when you go to the interview. It will not impress your interviewer if they request it and you cannot find it, it is wrinkled, or it has coffee spilled on it.

6. **Do ask basic questions.** Decide what additional information you would like to have before you go to the interview. Make a few notes for yourself and review them moments before: job description, salary, benefits, location, hours, etc. It is also okay to write down a few questions that you would like to ask and to take notes during the interview if you need to.

7. **Do be enthusiastic.** This does not mean that you are bouncing off the walls. It does mean that you are interested enough in this job to put your best foot forward and show that you care.

Interview Follow-up

Most people do not follow up with a company after their interview. Stand out in the crowd. Do a follow-up.

Within 24 hours of your interview, write a 'thank you' note.

Within 24 hours of your appointment, write a short note to the person who interviewed you and thank them for their time. Mention that you are very interested in their job (if you are) and that you will be looking forward to hearing from them in the near future. Also, offer to provide any additional information if they should decide that they need it.

Remember: 24 hours!

It is also permissible to call the company in a week or so to see if the job has been filled or whether they need additional information from you. You might want to ask the interviewer when an appropriate time would be to check back about this particular job. Diligent follow-up can sometimes make the difference in who gets a job and who doesn't.

If you have not heard from the company in a couple of months, it usually means that they hired someone else for that particular job. However, if you see that position advertised again, it may mean that they have additional positions open and you should resubmit your cover letter and resume. Most companies will keep resumes on file only a couple of months, assuming that within that length of time the applicant has probably taken another job and is no longer interested. If you care, let them know.

If you did not get the job that you applied for, it is appropriate for you to call and ask why. They may be willing to give you some excellent pointers that can help you land an even better job next time.

H.E.L.P. (Help Eliminate Long Pauses)

Go to www.howtogetandkeepajob.com for free work pages:
Sample resumes
Cover letter form
Referral list form
Contact form

CHAPTER 2
Why Do I Need to Make a Good Impression?

Sometimes in the winds of change,
we find our true direction.

Author unknown

It's winter, and your septic tank is clogged, and you know what a mess it is going to be to dig it up through the ice and snow, to have it repaired. However, you don't go without a septic tank, even in the winter. So, you call a repair man.

The first man shows up in a suit and tie. He has a gold earring in one ear and a large diamond on his hand. His shoes are highly polished and of the latest style. You can't help but notice his manicured nails and gold watch.

The second guy is wearing dirty jeans with his boxer shorts hanging out. His dirty shoes leave marks on your carpet, and you didn't want to shake hands with him. He is late.

The third guy has on jeans, but they are clean. His shirt is nicely pressed, even if it has seen a day or two of wear. His sturdy work shoes are obviously well worn, but he carefully wiped his feet before entering your home. He is wearing a watch; he has a pager and a notebook.

Do first impressions count? You bet!

Who would you most likely choose to do your septic tank work? Why?

Most people would choose the third guy. The first one was certainly not dressed for the type of work he was supposed to be doing. The second appeared sloppy and inconsiderate, which makes you think that his work might also be sloppy, and he might be difficult to work with.

The third has not just walked out of the pit, but he obviously knew what kind of clothes to wear for the type of work he was in. His watch and pager gave the impression that he was aware of the needs and time constraints of his customers. The fact that his hands were clean and he wiped his shoes indicated that he was thoughtful and courteous. He had a notebook. Apparently he was ready to record your particular needs and offer you a bid.

Do first impressions count? You bet.

Why Should I Want People to Notice Me?

Whether you are living in a time when the unemployment rate is hovering around ten percent or when the global economy is soaring, you want the best job that you can get. When the unemployment rate is soaring, it may be that any job is good enough. When it is not, you may be a little more selective.

It is basically the same. You are competing for the job you have chosen to acquire, and if you do not stand out in the crowd, you will be overlooked. It is just that simple.

How Do I Get People to Notice Me?

Whether you are looking for a job as a ditch digger or a CEO, an important part of your first impression is your behavior. If you are rude, vulgar, or unpleasant, you will immediately leave a bad first impression. If you are kind, courteous, and thoughtful, you will stand out in the crowd. If you think someone is not watching, think again.

Joanne Wallace is a professional speaker. She writes and does seminars for Christian women. One of her most famous stories is of the time when she was traveling from the East Coast to the West Coast and got stuck in the infamous Chicago O'Hare airport because of a late connecting flight. She rushed to the counter to inquire what she would have to do to get on another flight so that she could make the speaking engagement deadline that was scheduled.

The gentleman at the counter didn't even look up. He just simply told her that there would not be another flight for five hours. Her immediate impulse, as she tells it, was to get mad and maybe even say, "Do you know who I am?" and then she remembered who she really was. She has spent her life sharing with people how to be kind and thoughtful and be an exemplifier of a Christian woman. After saying a quick little prayer, she simply said, "Do you know where I can find a telephone?" and walked away.

Three hours later, after Joanne had covered all of the shops and sights in the airport terminal, she went in to have a cup of coffee and to wait out her final couple of hours. As she was sitting at the table, the young man who had given her the bad news of the five hour delay, rushed over to her. He said that he had been looking everywhere for her. She excitedly asked him if he had found an earlier flight, but he said no. When she asked him why he was looking for her, he told her this story.

He had, for some time, been curious about Christianity. He had talked with a few people and listened to some radio and TV shows, but he wanted to find something that was more than just hype. He wanted to find something that was real…something that was more than just talk. When Joanne walked up to his counter, he recognized her, and as he briskly told her that she would have to wait five hours for a new flight, he was testing her. He wanted to know if she would walk her talk.

She does, and she did. What a difference that day may have made in the life of that young man and all of the thousands of people over the years that have heard that story. I have never forgotten it, and every time I ran into a delay or a challenging situation when I was on the road lecturing—and even now—I try to remember that what I do or say may not only make a difference in my life, it may make a difference in someone else's life as well.

How to Show Off Your Talents

You have a multitude of talents. Some of them you may not even recognize. Take a moment and look at them. Do you have special skills that you have developed over the years for a particular job? These should show up on your resume. But, what other talents do you have? How about these:

- You get along well with people.
- You supervise people effectively and have done so through many volunteer efforts.
- You have the ability to motivate others.
- You are well organized and have used these skills not only in a professional setting but also in both volunteer work and/or in running a home.
- You are good at learning new skills.
- You are good at teaching new skills.
- You meet people easily.
- You make a good first impression.
- You write well.
- You speak well.
- You are willing to do what it takes to get a job done.
- You know how to network.

- You have done a variety of volunteer jobs in your church and/or community.

- You are aware of time and how important it is to others.

- You are self-disciplined.

- You hold yourself accountable for your actions.

- You know how to stay focused.

- You are willing to stick with a job until it is complete.

- You are a good listener.

- You are enthusiastic.

You have a multitude of talents.

These are just a few of the many things that you may have learned over the years by just living your life. People say that they have no skills because they have done nothing but go to school or be a stay-at-home mom or dad. That is not true! You cannot complete your education or run a home without accumulating numerous skills that can easily be transferred into the work force. Do not put yourself down. Think about what you have learned, make a list of it, and use it to get a job.

Why Would I Want and Need to be
Recognized in a New Environment?

Have you ever heard the saying "If you always do what you have always done, you will always get what you've always got"?

There is your answer. If you are not willing to step out of your comfort zone, you will never find the new and exciting opportunities that may be waiting for you just around the corner.

When I was five years old, my mother provided me with elocution lessons. In case you don't recognize that older word, it is speech lessons. I had to learn to say things like, "Rubber baby buggy bumper" and, "She sells sea shells by the sea shore. If she sells sea shells by the sea shore, where are the sea shells she sells by the sea shore?" Believe me, those are not only hard to say, they are even hard to write. Elocution is a little more than just a speech class. You learn a great deal of enunciation.

At least I learned at an early age how not to be frightened on a stage, and as a result, I spent many, many years on one through high school and college drama and speech clubs. I even taught communication skills at the college level for more years than I choose to remember.

One day I decided that I should do this for a living. I wanted to become a professional speaker. My kids were about grown, and I had the support of my family if I needed to travel, so they all told me to go for it. I thought that since I had been speaking all of my life it would be an easy thing to accomplish. Wrong!

I applied to do contract work with a national seminar company. They asked me about my public speaking skills. They wanted to know what I had done to polish the skills that I had acquired. I had done nothing. So, I began to look around for a place to work on those skills.

Be willing to step out of your comfort zone
to accomplish your goals.

I heard about the professional speaking division of Toastmasters International that was located in my city. I went to the meeting and told them that I, too, wanted to become a professional speaker. They were gentle but not overly encouraging when they told me that I would have to go through the entire program of Toastmasters in order to become a member of their club and that it could take years. I asked where to start.

In their program you have to go through a series of speeches in order to reach each level of speaking. Each speech is designed to teach you a specific technique, and it is an excellent program. You do, however, have to get on the speaking roster for the club in order to make your required speeches. I knew that I could never accomplish what I wanted to do in one club unless I was willing to donate several years to the process. I wasn't. So, I contacted every club within reasonable driving range of our city and asked to be placed on their speaking schedule, and I went to work. I completed the entire program in about six months.

Needless to say, the professional club was a little surprised when I walked back in six months later with all of my credentials for membership. So was the seminar company when I showed them my list of speaking engagements, my credentials, and the honors I had received.

Yes, I was out of my comfort zone, but I wanted to accomplish this goal, and I was willing to do what it took to get there.

This can be your story too. Never shoot for the stars, you may end up in the mud, but if you shoot for the moon, you might just end up in the stars.

Why Would I Want an Opportunity to Meet New People?

My new speaking abilities led me to a contract with a national seminar company, which gave me the opportunity to meet many, many new people all over the world. These contacts not only provided numerous opportunities for me, but they also provided me with a multitude of new friends, many with whom I am still in contact.

When I need information to complete a writing assignment, I usually have a contact to help me. When I need to learn a new skill, I will usually have someone who can help me or who will know someone to introduce me to. This is called networking.

If you want to get a job, and if you ever want more than to just have a "job," you absolutely must network. Join clubs, get involved in church work, volunteer in the community, and even get to know your neighbors. You never know when that new friend may some day be just the person you need for that special reference or source of information.

H.E.L.P.

Go to www.howtogetandkeepajob.com for free work pages:
Impression plan work sheet

CHAPTER 3
What Does it Take to Make
a Good First Impression?

How is what you do every day
making someone's life better?
That is your very important work.

Author unknown

Remember the septic tank guy? What impressed you about the one you would have hired? Was it the confident way he stood, looked at you, shook your hand, dressed, or spoke? Was it the way he focused on you and made you feel important, or was it the way he listened and completed the job in the manner in which you had requested? Maybe it was all of these things. You see, a good impression is not created by any one thing. It is a combination of traits that create that positive first impression, the one you want to present. Remember, people cannot see your credentials, they can only see you.

Ten Essential Traits

Here are ten traits that you need to be aware of if you want to make a good first impression. These are equally as important whether you are trying to get a job, keep a job, turn it into a career, or maybe even get a date.

1. **Nonverbal Communication:** There are three ways we communicate: verbally, nonverbally, and through writing. Ninety-five percent of the way you communicate is nonverbal. Your image is created by the way you stand, the way you dress, and by the way you respond to others. When you have

poor posture, keep your hands, arms and legs close to your body and avoid eye contact, you are usually perceived by others as someone with poor self-esteem and therefore a lack of self-confidence. The opposite: good posture, a relaxed body, good eye contact, and a good handshake give the impression of self-confidence and inspire others to believe in you. Marilyn Maple, a former professor of education at the University of Florida, said, "Body language is the oldest, most trusted language in the world."

Ninety-five percent of the way you communicate is nonverbal.

2. **Good Posture:** "Good posture identifies you as someone with something to say," said Lynn Pearl, past president of Executive Communication, Inc. When you have good posture, you will be standing or sitting erectly. You do not slump or lean on the nearest object. Place your feet slightly apart to give you good balance. If you are standing for any length of time, bend your knees slightly like they do in the band or in the military. Keep your hands to the side or in front, but do not create a "fig leaf" in the front of your slacks or skirt. If you can't figure out what to do with you hands and are terribly uncomfortable, keep something in them. It could be your resume, a business card, your briefcase, or a purse (if you are a lady). Do not stuff your hands in your pockets. Do not cross your arms as this indicates a "closed" attitude. Practice this stance so that you can become comfortable in your own body and won't look totally awkward.

3. **Handshake:** There is nothing much worse than a wimpy handshake to destroy a good impression. It can give you cold chills up and down your spine. *Never*

ever give anyone a wimpy handshake…never, never, never! There are several basic rules for handshakes:

a. Always stand when shaking hands.

b. Always shake hands with your right hand even if the other person is unable to use their right hand.

c. If you need to cough or sneeze, cover your mouth with your left hand.

d. If you have sweaty palms, don't rub them on your clothes or use a tissue. You might pass the tissue on to the other person. It is better to use a colorless and odorless antiperspirant on your hand.

e. You may shake hands with gloves on, but it is better to remove them first.

f. To be sure that you do not receive a wimpy handshake, slightly push your hand into the hand of the receiver because that way, they cannot grab your fingers first.

g. Give your acquaintances a firm handshake, but do not break their hand. Sometimes people have arthritis in their hands and a handshake that is too hard can be very painful. This is to be a pleasant encounter, not a painful memory.

h. Never ignore someone who has offered to shake your hand.

The handshake is a very strong form of nonverbal communication.

The handshake is a very strong form of nonverbal communication and tells you a lot about the other person. Ask several people if you have a good handshake. If they hesitate with their answer, then maybe you need to work on it.

4. **Eye Contact:** "Eye contact is the most remembered element in forming an impression," said Nancy Austin, co-author of *A Passion for Excellence.* Five to seven seconds is a good length of time for direct eye contact. Anything longer becomes a stare. When you are shaking hands—right hand to right hand—your eyes will naturally go to their left eye. You cannot look someone in both eyes at the same time. Your eyes come to a point to focus. If you look at one eye, rather than shifting from one eye to the other, you have a much better chance of holding that person's attention. It is very difficult to look away from someone who is looking at one of your eyes. Try it. You will be surprised.

5. **Focusing:** Small talk and general conversations are an integral part of conducting business. Sharing common experiences and developing knowledge of mutual interests can build trust and help you forge good relationships with business associates and clients. However, it can be detrimental. If you allow yourself to get off track too much of the time, it will quickly become evident that you have the inability to focus and therefore will not be responsible to handle an important job or one with a short deadline. Learn to put other things and thoughts away when necessary and accomplish what needs to be done, when it needs to be done.

6. **Conversations:** When you do have an opportunity to talk with clients (those who buy your services), customers (those who buy your products), or your boss (the one who signs your paycheck), be thoughtful of what you say. A good conversationalist is generally well read and can converse on many issues. You do not have to be all knowledgeable, but you need to stay aware of what is going on around you and in this global society. Listen to the news,

read the summaries on the front page of the *Wall Street Journal*, read book reviews, and occasionally check out the *National Geographic* magazine to broaden your horizons about other cultures.

There are also don'ts, or topics that you should avoid in most all situations:

a) Gossip

b) Your health

c) Controversial social issues

d) Political campaign issues

e) Religion

f) Sex

g) Profanity

h) Inappropriate jokes

i) Personal problems

Above all, use good grammar. It does not matter what type of job you are looking for: nothing says more about your education and the pride you have in your own abilities than your ability to use correct grammar. If you missed it in school, study it now. It is never too late.

Clients buy your services, customers buy your products. Bosses sign your paycheck.

7. **Listening:** According to Jim Duggar in *Listen Up: Hear What's Really Being Said,* there are seven reasons why you should want to be a better listener:

a. Listening improves communication.

b. Listening puts you in control of the situation.

c. Listening lessens arguments.

d. Listening shows that you care.

e. Listening helps you better understand your world.

f. Listening can improve your memory.

g. Listening makes you a better manager, employee, spouse, friend, parent, etc.

There is a difference between listening and hearing. Hearing is a physical ability, and listening is a skill. Listening skills give you the ability to know what someone is talking about. If you are truly interested in improving this skill, learn how to sit still when someone is talking, maintain good eye contact, and don't interrupt. Sometimes even leaning toward the speaker or nodding your head will make the speaker feel as though you are making contact. If you are biased or prejudiced toward the speaker or the subject, it can become an immediate barrier to your ability to listen. Your attention span can also create a barrier to listening. Worry, fear, anger, noise, or even accents can become barriers quite easily.

Hearing is a physical ability, listening is a skill.

If you have children, then you know what it is like to talk to the wall. That is how it feels to talk to many employees. Be different. Exhibit your ability to listen, and you will stand out in the crowd.

8. **A Professional Look:** Do interviewers really form an opinion about you based on the way you dress? Yes, they do. Experts say that the biggest challenge that they have is finding people who are willing to dress for success. You may be a

nonconformist, but when you are at work or looking for a job, you need to be a part of the team. Your goal is to project a professional image regardless of your employment or career path choice.

Unless your job requires a uniform, choosing clothing that is appropriate for work may be difficult. When going for an interview at a particular company, you might want to drive by as the employees are coming or going one day and observe what they are wearing. You may adhere to their dress code, but for the interview you should always dress slightly better than you would if you were already an employee. In other words, take it up a notch.

The styles, lengths, colors, and the fit of your clothing speak volumes about your ability to do your job. The goal should be to "look professional." In other words, if someone were to ask what you had on, the answer should be, "I don't remember, but he/she looked good." You never want someone to say, "All I remember about him was that large belt buckle," or, "All I remember about her were those bright red shoes." Not a good way to make a good first impression.

Let's look at the ladies first:

a. Dress like the highest level female in your organization. Does she wear skirt suits or pant suits? How about hose and open-toed shoes? If there is no female role model, then check on the style of the men's clothing. Do they wear suits and ties, or are they more casual?

b. Traditional career colors are navy (trustworthy), gray (conservative), and black (chic). Most of these colors will work well in skirt suits or pant suits, and when teamed with a softer feminine color for a blouse, you can easily obtain a very professional look.

c. Your shoes and hose should match the bottom of your skirt or pants. This keeps the bottom part of your look dark and creates a focal point around your face, which is where you want people to be looking.

d. Be sure your shoes are well polished and do not have run-down or scuffed heels. Of course, always have an extra pair of hose handy in case of a run.

e. Be sure that your clothes fit. Clothes that are too small or too large just simply look tacky.

f. Skirts and shirts that are too short or too revealing are out of place. When you sit, your skirt should hit or cover your knee. Shirts should cover the belly and shoulders and, please, remember that undergarments belong under garments.

g. Keep your clothes neat, clean, and pressed.

h. Your nails should be a reasonable length, neat, and clean.

i. If your hair has not been styled since you got out of high school or college or in the last several years, find a good hairdresser and ask for a professional style that suits your type of business.

Undergarments belong under garments.

j. The same is true of your makeup. If you have not changed your makeup style in the last few years, go to a department store and get a free makeover, or contact a cosmetics specialist and ask for an updated style. Wherever you go, your makeup should be tasteful and subtle.

k. Wearing your best is not always a good idea for an interview, especially if your best is a cocktail dress.

l. For best results, wear **no** fragrances.

m. Jewelry that jangles is very distracting, not only for an interview, but also in an office atmosphere. Choose your jewelry carefully, sparingly, and tastefully.

n. Slouchy handbags look sloppy. Choose a style that will give you an organized image. If you carry it on your shoulder, use the left shoulder so that it does not fall down if someone should offer you a handshake.

o. In the casual atmosphere or for casual days, remember that casual does not mean sloppy. Khakis and a sport shirt or a nice sweater might work, but jeans, shorts, t-shirts, hats, and sneakers won't hack it.

p. Take one last look in a full-length mirror before you walk out of the house. Remember, an inappropriate outfit can do permanent damage to your professional image.

Now how about the guys:

a. Wrinkled, even under a jacket, is apparent. And, yes, people do notice wrinkled pants.

b. Dirty, damaged, and scuffed shoes are not acceptable. And, oh yes, **no white socks** with a suit, and no tennis shoes.

c. Be sure that your clothes fit. They should be neither too loose nor too tight. Please do not wear a tie around a collar that you cannot button or wear pants that are too short.

d. Too casual can destroy your professional image. If you would feel comfortable wearing this particular outfit to a ballgame or to the beach, it is definitely wrong for an interview.

e. You need at least one conservative and well-styled suit in your wardrobe. Check with the men's department of a good department store and let them help you design a professional look that is good for you.

f. Be sure that your hair, nails, and body are clean. If you have not had your hair styled in several year—or ever—find a good barber and ask for a professional look that fits with your new lifestyle.

g. Keep your beard, if you have one, well trimmed and in an appropriate style. If you are clean shaven, then keep it that way.

h. Regardless of whether it is a designated casual day or not, if you have guests coming to your office, dress professionally.

i. Dress for the job you want.

Dress for the job you want!

After these long lists, you are probably asking if all of this really matters. The answer is a resounding, "**Yes!**" A friend of mine was telling about his daughter recently. He said that she was looking for a new job and came by his office after a long day of checking on possibilities. She was very frustrated because she had not been able to land one interview. He said that he looked at her and said, "Honey, look in the mirror and try again tomorrow." She had on sloppy, torn jeans, a midriff top with a crop jacket, and was carrying an enormous brightly colored bag.

The next afternoon his daughter rushed into the office and said, "Dad, I got a job!" He was thrilled for her but not surprised since she had on a black pantsuit with black heels—all neatly pressed and polished. She had fixed her hair in a very flattering manner and was carrying a small and very professional looking handbag. Yes, appearance does make a difference.

A couple of last notes: If you have tattoos and/or body jewelry, be sure that they are covered until you know whether they are acceptable in that particular organization. And, **no cell phones!** Please have the courtesy to at least leave your cell phone on vibrate when you are in an interview. In fact, you should never have your cell phone turned on at work unless you are expecting a death message, a message about a transplant, or your wife is imminently expecting. You can check your messages during lunch or on your break. Help your family and friends understand.

9. **Organization:** How organized are you? Were you late for this job interview? Did you forget it and have to reschedule? Did you get lost on your way? Good organizational skills are a key to maintaining a successful career, and they are apparent to a good interviewer from the very beginning.

Ask yourself some basic questions, and if the answer is "Yes" to any of them, it is time to resolve some of your organizational challenges:

    a. Do you spend too much time on basic tasks?

    b. Do you miss deadlines because you do not allocate the right amount of time for the project?

    c. Are your files so unorganized that you have difficulty accessing them quickly?

    d. Are you feeling overwhelmed by too much paperwork?

    e. Do you accept more work than you can handle?

If any of these are challenges to you, then it is time to learn some basic organizational skills. If you choose not to do so, you will jeopardize your job and any career opportunities that you might have, because you will miss appointments and deadlines and lose valuable material. Your problem-solving abilities will decrease, and stress will create an unpleasant atmosphere not only for you, but also for your co-workers.

Be enthusiastic!

10. **Enthusiasm:** Enthusiasm comes from the Greek word *entheos*, which means "God within." It is the basis of who you are and how you approach your life. When you can become self-confident enough to look enthusiastically at others—and be happy about what they are doing and accomplishing—then you will have reached a level of life in which you have given yourself the blessing of enthusiasm. When you reach the point where you can focus on the message and not the messenger, then you will be overtaken by enthusiasm. When you can become so passionate about a project, an idea, or a creation that you are compelled to share it, life becomes a continuous reward and you will truly understand what it is like to have "God within." Life will become infectious and such fun to share that each day will be a new, bright, and exciting experience.

It will reflect who you are.

H.E.L.P.

Go to www.howtogetandkeepajob.com for free work pages:
Personal evaluation form

Section II
How to Keep a Job

Your earning ability today is largely dependent upon your knowledge, skill and your ability to combine that knowledge and skill in such a way that you contribute value for which customers are going to pay.

Brian Tracy

What are They Looking For?

What are most companies looking for? They are looking for a package deal. They want someone who can put it all together. In other words, they are looking for:

Professional dress

Referral techniques

Organizational abilities

First Impressions

Esteem—good, that is

Stress management

Skills like writing, listening, computers, etc.

Interview abilities

Opportunity networks

New ideas

Attitude—positive

Laughter—the best medicine

Importance of goals

Self-management

Money management

Most companies have plenty of choices in employees, so to not only get a job but also to keep a job and turn it into a career, you must learn how to be on the competitive edge. You must learn that some things are more important than payday and 5 o'clock. When you become involved with your work and give it your all, it will become evident to those who are watching. And they are watching.

This does not mean that you must become a workaholic. Actually that can be as much a detriment as it is an asset. It can indicate that you are not sufficiently organized to accomplish your work in the designated amount of time. Or it could indicate that you are not a good time manager. Or, as a manager, it could indicate that you are not good at delegating.

We are going to talk about all of these issues. In this section we will deal specifically with these skills:

1) Attitude

2) Goal Setting

3) Assertion versus Aggression

4) Creative Communication Skills

5) Time Management

6) Leadership

7) Budgeting and

8) Stress Management.

To keep a job you want, you must become "The Package." You must have it all together and be willing and determined to continue improving it.

Notes

CHAPTER 4
Skill No. 1 - Attitude

He who angers you, controls you.

Author unknown

How Is Your Attitude?

Several years ago when I was a full-time international lecturer, I received a call from a corporation that was considering me as the keynote speaker for their annual meeting. They asked for a video clip of my presentation. I told them that I would be happy to provide it and immediately popped a tape into the dub machine to get a copy of the prepared speech.

Somehow, and to this day, I have no idea how, the machine was connected to the TV, and instead of copying my prepared presentation, it taped a current show… one similar to the Jerry Springer show.

I mailed the tape.

In a few days, I received a call from one of the corporate officers asking me why I had sent them that particular tape. He said, "We watched the entire tape and never did see you. Were you a guest or what?" Needless to say, I was horrified. I apologized so sincerely that I even drove to their corporate office—out of town—and apologized again and hand delivered the new tape.

Choose to laugh and learn.

Of course, the damage was done, and I did not get the job, but I learned a very valuable lesson. You **never** send out a sample of your work without checking it first.

This could have been a devastating point in my career, but instead I chose to laugh about it, share it, and help others learn a precious lesson.

In most situations in life, you can either laugh or cry, and it is a lot more pleasant for everyone and a lot more fun to laugh. My philosophy has always been that if it is going to be funny in five years, it might as well be funny now.

When I was on the lecture circuit, I tried to help the audiences understand this concept by telling them that if I accidentally stepped off the front of the stage (and some of them were quite high) that day, it would be sad and maybe physically devastating for at least a while. But, I can promise you, that when they told the story in years to come, they would laugh. So why not laugh today?

I did my share of funny things like dropping blush on my white skirt, "so I could share with them what color I was wearing," and picking up the black mascara instead of the lip gloss and touching up my lips without a mirror.

If I had not been able to laugh at myself, I would have cried a lot.

Importance of a Good Attitude

Experts tell us that success is 20% perspiration and 80% attitude. I am not sure how accurate those numbers are, but I do know that a good attitude can make a huge difference between actually enjoying what you are doing and only tolerating it. An apparent good attitude can also make the difference between being given the opportunity for a job and/or advancement and maybe an increase in your paycheck and in not having one at all.

It is estimated that 60% of all workers are unhappy with their jobs. If you are one of those 60%, you need to be very careful because it can easily carry over to your personal and family time and create a negative effect on your overall life.

Give yourself a simple and quick check-up: Take a piece of paper and draw a line from the top to the bottom through the middle of the page. On the left hand side of the paper, write down all the things that you hate about your job. On the right side of the paper, write down all the good things about your job. Be honest. Look carefully at the list. If the right side outweighs the left side, then maybe you don't need to be looking for a job at all. Maybe you just need to change your attitude about the one you already have.

You are never going to find the perfect job. Of course, they are not going to find the perfect employee in you either. Sometimes you win, and sometimes you don't. The difference between the two is that if you are a winner, you will get up and try again *every* time you get knocked down. If you are a loser, you will just lie there and feel sorry for yourself.

How Do You Get and Maintain a Good Attitude?

Think of the people in your life—whether at work, at the employment office, or in your personal life—that you look at and envy because they seem to have it all together. You have wished so many times that you could be just like them. Well, you can. The truth is, they are no different from you. They have challenges on a daily basis just like you. They have had times when they have been afraid that they were going to lose their job. They have had times when they desperately needed a job or at least a new one. They have had times when they were challenged by the things that were going on in their personal lives. They are just like you. We all are.

The difference between them and you is attitude. Those people whom you envy because they seem to have it all together have chosen to get back up one more time and believe in who they are and what they can accomplish. This, too, can be your choice.

What Is a Self-Fulfilling Prophecy?

There is a theory known as the self-fulfilling prophecy. It goes something like this: what you honestly believe, expect, and tell yourself about your life, will happen.

For example, if you have finally found the job you want, put together a great resume and cover letter, and landed the interview, you are on your way. If, however, you walk into that interview saying to yourself, "He is never going to hire me. I am not good enough for this job," the chances are that you will be right. He won't hire you.

There is something about the negative self-talk that seems to emanate from you towards others so that they pick up on your emotions. When you walk into an interview with that kind of attitude, it is like the interviewer can "hear" what you have been saying to yourself and they, too, will begin to think that you are not good enough for the job.

On the other hand, if you will do a little—or a lot—of positive self-talk before the interview and say things like, "This job is mine. They cannot wait to hire me. I am definitely the best person for this job," then your positive attitude will be apparent in your presence. People want to hire employees who exhibit that kind of confidence.

I know, it sounds a little weird. But it works. You will find out more about how to use affirmations a little later in this book, but suffice it to say at this point, positive self-talk is one of the sanest things that you can do.

When I was on the lecture circuit, I had to be my best every day. I was not allowed to have a bad day. People were paying big bucks to hear me speak, and they did not care whether I had had any sleep the night before. They did not care that my plane had been caught in a snow storm, and I did not get in until 6 AM. They did not care that my motel room had caught on fire, and I had no clothes to wear except the Levi jumpsuit that I traveled in. (Actually both of these things did happen.) All they wanted was their money's worth of my time.

When you are in an office and lose your voice or throw up all night, you can call in sick. If I woke up with no voice that morning, I was expected to just hold the microphone a little closer and get through the day *and* give an excellent presentation. I didn't always feel like it. So, what did I do?

On the way to the lecture hall every morning, I would say as loudly as I could get by with, "I am the best! I am the best! I am the best!" over and over again. If I was having a bad day, I might start saying it in the bathroom as I was combing my hair. When I was back stage waiting to go on, sometimes I would jump up and down to get my adrenaline pumped up a little. You see, if I had not had much sleep, the adrenal gland was not working really well, and if I didn't get excited, the audience would have gone to sleep, too.

"I am the best!" "I am the best!" "I am the best!"

It is important that you not only believe in yourself but also that you visualize what you are worth. If I could not visualize an excellent performance or presentation for that day, then I would not give one. The same is true for your new job or promotion. If you cannot see yourself working at that job or being worthy of that promotion or increased salary level, it will not happen.

If you want a new house, get a picture of it and put it on your wall. If you want an increase in salary, then take one of your current paychecks, photocopy it, change the amount to your desired level, and post it in a private place in your office, on your refrigerator, or on the bathroom mirror. It must be someplace where you will see it often.

The vision of that item will begin to program your subconscious mind, and once it sees it over and over again, the subconscious mind will begin to make that action happen. Your subconscious mind only takes orders, and once it is programmed to do something, it cannot do anything except make it happen. The subconscious mind has no ability to analyze or make judgments: it just performs.

You will learn a great deal more about this when we get into goal setting in a later chapter. Right now, take my word for it—it happens.

As I became more and more successful on the lecture circuit, it became apparent that my income was going to rapidly increase to an amount that I had never even dreamed of. However, I knew that if I could not see myself being worthy of that amount of money, I would somehow sabotage my efforts, and it would not happen. I didn't think that was a good idea because I really liked the idea of making that kind of money at least once in my life.

I did as I just suggested to you. I took a commission check, photocopied it, and changed the numbers to, what I considered at that point, a ridiculous sum of money. I put it in my briefcase. I would look at it every night before I went to bed, and I would look at it every morning before I went to the conference room. Before long I began to believe that I really was worth that kind of money. And it happened.

Visualize your worth and grow into it.

The first time I actually received a commission check for what I had previously considered to be a ridiculous sum of money, I thought, "Oh, is that all. I think I will change it to a larger amount." You see, I had become worthy of that kind of salary and because I believed it, I had begun to perform at that level of excellence as well.

Focus on the Bright Side of Life

It takes fewer muscles to smile than it does to frown. So why do you want to frown? If you are using that many more muscles, you are also using more energy. Don't you have something better to do with all of that energy?

Everyone has a sense of humor. Some people just choose not to use it. Life is so much easier if you choose to focus your energy on the good things of life and choose to enjoy life a little more.

Most people who have a good sense of humor also have a positive attitude. They do not let the little everyday annoyances rule their life. Most situations we find ourselves in are not life and death issues. When you have a challenging experience, stop and ask yourself how you are going to feel about this experience in five years. If you think it might, just might, be humorous, then let's laugh about it now. Some people take everything so seriously that they can't even enjoy the experiences that can be fun.

A number of years ago, we bought a house that had atrocious wallpaper in it. The kitchen paper was huge silver poinsettias, and the paper in the girls' bathroom looked like something that had come off the box of a bad scent of men's cologne. It was some green and blue plaid thing. As we walked into the house with the first box on moving day, I put it down and began ripping wallpaper off the kitchen wall. My husband said, "What are you doing?" I told him that no paper was better than that paper, and I would rather look at a blank wall.

It didn't take long for my daughter and me to head to the wallpaper store. We spent several hours looking through the books, and then I told the salesperson that I wanted to order this paper for the kitchen, this paper for the bathroom, and this paper for the hall. She said, "You mean you want to take the books home and see how it would look in your rooms." I told her, "No, I want to order the paper." She gave me this very strange look and said, "Nobody ever orders the paper the first time they come in."

I was amazed. This was not a life and death decision. We were just buying wallpaper. If it didn't work out, someday we would replace it.

Most decisions are just not worth the amount of anxiety that we allow them to sap from our energy. Make a concerted effort to look for humor in simple things, and make it a habit. One of the great blessings of humor is that it does not allow you to take yourself too seriously, and no one expects you to be perfect anyway, so stop trying.

Studies have shown that people who can have fun at work:

    a. **Enjoy their work more.**

    b. **Have less stress in their lives.**

    c. **Are far more creative.**

    d. **Are highly motivated.**

    e. **Are ill much less frequently.**

No, you cannot become a brain surgeon by saying that you are one. But if you have the talent, are willing to do what it takes, and believe in yourself, you will have a much better chance of succeeding than you would by simply saying, "I will never make it."

11 Steps to Have a PMA (Positive Mental Attitude)

All right, let's summarize: If you are unhappy in your life, it will show up in all aspects of your life. It can prevent you from finding and/or keeping the job you want and deserve. A negative mental attitude can affect you both emotionally and physically and will sabotage your dreams and desires.

A positive mental attitude is essential for overall well-being and success in life and work - even if you are in a negative environment.

What can you do to make this happen?

1. **Be grateful.** Scripture reminds us to be grateful "in" all things, not necessarily "for" all things. There is a difference. However, if the difference

confuses you, just be grateful. Be grateful for what you have, for who you are, and what you are being given. Be kind, be thoughtful, look for the good in all things, keep a smile on your face, and start each day by saying thank you for life and another day. It is amazing how a change of actions can change your attitude.

Choose to have fun in everything you do.

2. **Keep your life well balanced.** It is important that you keep all areas of your life well balanced. When one is out of balance, it can throw another area out of balance. It is much like having a flat spot on a tire. It will not run smoothly with one part out of balance.

3. **Never give up.** Probably the most famous speech that Winston Churchill ever gave was the one where he said, "Never, never, never, never…never give in." Always get up one more time than you fall down.

4. **Make the best of everything.** Whatever situation you happen to be in, look for the silver lining. There is good in everything. Sometimes it is very challenging to find, but we can always learn and grow from every situation.

5. **Use positive self-talk.** Don't ever talk down to yourself. You are your own best friend; you always have been and always will be. Be kind to yourself and treat yourself with the respect of a best friend.

6. **Visualize your dreams.** What you think about, you can bring about. If you do not see it, you cannot have it. Your dreams are the hopes of tomorrow.

7. **First things first.** If you see a problem and/or accidentally create one, deal with it. Don't postpone it until it festers. Turn your lemons into lemonade.

8. **Look for the good.** Most of the time in life, you will find what you are looking for. If you expect to find a bad situation, you will usually not be disappointed. If you expect to find a good situation, it, too, will be there.

9. **Look for humor.** Don't take yourself too seriously. Learn to laugh at yourself and **with** others but—**never at them.**

10. **Make work fun.** Be creative. Challenge yourself into contests to succeed and win. When I decided to write this book, I set a goal of writing it in 28 days. It was my goal, and it kept me on track. It also kept me from getting frustrated and walking away or getting distracted and not getting it done. I did it, and it was fun.

11. **Keep on Growing.** You either grow or you lose your abilities. It is impossible to stand still in life. If I quit writing, I will lose my ability to put thoughts together in a smooth and flowing manner. The more I work at it, the better I will become.

A positive mental attitude will not change any negative situation you find yourself in, but it can help you deal more effectively with what you are experiencing until you can make it better. Make life work for you. It can, but it is your choice. Do you want life—home, family, job—to become better every day, or do you want it to become stagnant? It is your decision and…no one else's.

H.E.L.P.

Go to www.howtogetandkeepajob.com for free work pages:
Self-evaluation form

CHAPTER 5
Skill No. 2 – Goal Setting

Live with intention! Plant your goals in your mind.

Author unknown

Are Goals Really Worth It?

Do you know where you want to be in five years? Do you know where you want to be in ten years? Do you know where you want to be next week?

It has been said that most of us have both short-term and long-term goals. However, for some people, a short-term goal is to get out of bed in the morning, and the long-term goal is simply to stay up all day.

If you don't know where you are going, you're probably going to end up somewhere else.

If you don't know where you are going, you're probably going to end up somewhere else.

Let's say when you get home this evening that you get a phone call and the person on the phone says, "Congratulations! You and your family have just won an all-expenses-paid trip anywhere in the world that you want to go, *if* you can be at the airport and ready to leave by 7 o'clock in the morning."

Assume that this is a legitimate phone call. Could you be ready and at the airport by 7 o'clock in the morning? Could you actually have all of those major projects taken care of, the packing done, the kids arranged to get out of school, all of the family errands run, the household chores completed and all the arrangements made for the pets and be packed and at the airport by 7 AM? Most of us probably could under the circumstances.

It's the next morning. We all jump into the car and dash to the airport. We are so excited as we run to the counter. The ticket agent says, "May I help you?" You say, "Yes, oh yes, yes, yes! My family has just won an all-expenses-paid trip to anywhere in the world that we want to go." "That's wonderful. Congratulations. Where would you like to go?" You stop and all look at each other. You have been so excited and so busy that you have made no decision as to where you want to go. You begin to talk with each other, and the first thing you know, the people in the line behind you are shuffling their feet and clearing their throats. They are showing some very obvious signs that you are in their way. Finally the ticket agent says, "Excuse me. I will be happy to send you anywhere you would like to go, but I need to know where that is. Would you mind stepping over to the side for just a few minutes and deciding where it is you want to go? When you come up with an idea, I will be glad to take care of you."

If you don't know where you are going, sometimes you can't go anywhere.

Not having goals in your life is like getting into your car, starting the engine, and never touching the steering wheel.

Goals are a plan.

Did you take a vacation last year? How long was it—a week, two weeks? Maybe it was just a long weekend. Think about what you did before you took that vacation. Didn't you sit down with the family or the significant people in your world and make plans? Didn't you talk about where you were going, when you were going to leave, how you were going to get there, what you were going to do, and when you were planning on coming back? Most people spend more time planning their vacations than they do their lives.

Goals are a plan. Goals are the way we get to where we want to go. They are the most valuable asset of our successful lives. A goal is anything that you can have, be, or do. Only 5 out of every 100 people actually set goals. Interestingly enough, research has confirmed that at age 65, only 5 out of every 100 people are able to financially take care of themselves. Coincidence? Most likely not.

In Mark McCormack's book *What They Don't Teach You At Harvard Business School*, he tells of a Harvard study conducted between 1979 and 1989. In 1979, the graduates of the MBA program were asked whether or not they had made and/or written down their goals. Three percent of the students had written goals. Thirteen percent had goals, but they were not in writing, and 84% had no specific goals at all.

Ten years later, in 1989, the researchers interviewed the members of that class again. They found that the 13% who had goals but not in writing were earning, on average, twice as much as the 84% who had no goals. However, the three percent who had made and written out their goals ten years before were now earning, on average, ten times as much as the other 97% of graduates all together.

Written goals do make a difference.

Basic Steps to Goal-Setting

1. You must have a beginning date. Have you ever noticed that "someday" is not a day in the week? Have you ever run into somebody down at the store and they say, "Come by and see me sometime." When do they expect you to show up? "I'm going back to school someday." When are you going to start?

I love the story of the man who said, "I'd love to go back and get a master's degree. I think it would be wonderful, but you know if I went back to school and worked on this master's degree and had to go at night, it would probably take me three years, and by the time I got through, I'd be 42 years old." The friend looked at the man and said, "How old will you be in three years if you don't go back to school?" We have to have a beginning date.

2. **Your goals need to be specific.** The more specific your goals, the more likely they are to happen. If you want a new home, write down everything you can think of about that home. Where is it going to be located? What does it look like? What color is it? What does the yard look like? Is it brick or stucco, or is it a log cabin? What color are the walls? What color are the floors? How are the rooms arranged? Write down as much detail as you can about this new home that you want. Get a picture if at all possible, and post it in an obvious location like on a mirror or the refrigerator door.

It works. The picture on our refrigerator ended up being our home for sixteen years.

If you want a new car, you need to know what kind it will be. What color is it? What model is it? What color is the interior? How big of an engine does it have? Be very, very specific about the details of that new car and, again, get a picture if you can, and post it in a very obvious location.

Do the same thing if you want a promotion. What promotion do you want? When do you want it? What kind of salary will you receive? What will your new office look like? What are you going to do with the extra income? How are you going to feel about this new level of responsibility? The more specific the goals, the more likely they are to happen. Post this information in your home office, and stick it in your briefcase or in a place where you will see it often.

A goal not written down is only a dream.

3. **The goals must be written down.** Unless your goals are written down, they are only a dream. There is something magic about writing down your goals. It

is almost like it says, "Oops! I am serious this time. I really mean it." When you write down your goals, stop and think about how you feel. Some of you may feel a sense of commitment. Some of you may feel a sense of relief. Some of you may feel a little bit scared because you have actually decided to do something about your life. Whatever the feelings, write them down and keep them beside your bed, posted in your office, on your bathroom mirror, or stick them in a frequently used spot in your briefcase. The point is to *look at them and read them out loud—often.* This is important. (You will learn more about exactly how to write these goals later in this chapter.)

   4. Your goals need to be committed to someone who believes in you. A lot of times we commit goals to people who are significant in our world: co-workers, people who are friends, or people who know us very well. That is not always the best idea. If they know us too well, they may try to protect us instead of keeping us on target.

   For example, say that you came to me and said, "Donna, I think I would like to learn to ride a bicycle. I never had a chance to ride a bicycle when I was a kid, and I always thought it would be fun." I am a very significant person in your world, and I know that you trip when you walk down the hall. I know that your coordination level is just not the best in the world. I might say, "Are you sure you want to do this? You might get hurt. Maybe you should think about this a little more. Maybe you should choose a goal that is a little safer for you." Isn't this what people do who are very close to you? Don't they back us off from our goals sometimes?

   You want to commit your goals to that person who says to you, "That's a great idea. I think it's wonderful that you want to learn how to ride that bike." Even when you fall and skin your knees, they are still there for you. "That's okay, that's just part of learning how to ride a bike. You are going to do it. I believe in you." You want to commit your goals to that person who believes in you anyway.

5. You want an ending date. Is that ending date in concrete? If you don't make that ending date, is somebody going to come get your kids, even if you'd like for them to? Does that mean that the sun will never shine again? Will the world end tomorrow if you don't make your goal? Of course not! The ending date is a target date, and if you don't make it, it is okay. Strive for it, work for it, but if you don't make it, just set another date and go on.

I have a friend who is a national sales director for a major company in America. She had to set her ending date five times before she made national. But she is there, and wasn't that the purpose? She made it.

I'd like to share a story with you which I found to be quite meaningful.

Three boys and their counselor came to a field of freshly fallen snow. No tracks marked the glistening surface. It was suggested that they have a contest to see who could walk the straightest line across the field.

The first boy began. He gazed down watching every step, trying to place one foot directly in front of the other. He looked neither up, nor back. When he finished crossing the field, he found that there were gradual but obvious curves in the path that he had made.

The second boy was determined to check himself from time to time, so he walked about 20 yards, paused, looked back, made an adjustment, walked 20 more yards, paused and looked back again. In this manner, he made his way to the other side of the field. When he saw the path that he had made, he found that he had many zigzags, veering to the left and then to the right.

The third boy tried to learn from the other two. He selected a large tree directly across the field and fixed his gaze upon it and walked straight ahead to it. He looked neither to his feet, nor did he look behind him. Fixing his eyes on the tree, he stepped confidently toward it. As you might have suspected, he walked the straightest path.

If you look back over the last five years of your life, and instead of seeing five years of progress, you see only one year of experience repeated five times, there is a message in this story for you, as there was for me.

It's not always easy to make goals happen. But persistence pays off. There was a study done about sales and persistence in which they determined that 80% of all sales are made on the fifth call. Forty-eight percent of the sales people give up after their first call. Twenty-five percent give up after their second call. Twelve percent make three calls and then stop. Five percent quit after the fourth call. The remaining ten percent keep on calling after the fourth call and to this persistent ten percent goes 80% of all sales. Be patient and persistent. It is worth it.

80% of all sales are made on the 5th call.

H. L. Hunt, a multi-billionaire who died in the late 1970s, was a bankrupt cotton farmer at the age of 32. Someone asked him what was required to be successful. He said there were two things that you must be willing to do to be successful. Number one, you have to decide exactly what you want. Number two, you have to determine the price you are willing to pay.

Why People Don't Set Goals

1. They don't understand the importance of goals. If you do not set goals, you end up living a life of extended mediocrity. People don't understand that if they want success, they have to plan for success. Scripture tells us, "As a man thinketh in his heart, so is he" (Proverbs 23:7, KJV). If he thinks he's going to be successful, he will be successful. Napoleon Hill said that whatever a man can think and believe, he can achieve.

2. People don't know how to set goals. We go to school anywhere from 12 to16 to19 years, and rarely during our educational experience are we taught how to set goals. That is a tragedy. We talk about success. We talk about achievement. We talk about the kind of things we want to have in our lives. We talk about where we want to go, but we rarely talk about how to get there.

3. They may have a fear of rejection. We're so afraid that someone is going to make fun of us, or that we are not going to be the person we claim to be or appear to be, so we refuse to set goals out of fear of rejection. If we don't set them, we can't fail. If we can't fail, people can't reject us for having failed.

4. They may have a fear of failure. One of the greatest obstacles to success in our adult lives is the fear of failure. Most of us have difficulty understanding that it is impossible to succeed without failure. Those in life who have reached the greatest successes are the ones who have failed the most.

Failure is simply falling forward. It takes time and experience to become successful. It is not a destination. Success is a journey. Often the greatest achievements that we have in life are accomplished after our greatest failures.

Look at Thomas Edison. He patented 1,097 different items. When he was working on the electric light, he had tried 5,000 different substances to make the filament. Someone came to him and said, "Mr. Edison, how come you keep going? You have already failed 5,000 times." To that Mr. Edison replied, "No, I haven't failed 5,000 times. I have just found 5,000 ways that won't work." Could you have kept trying?

Would you have tried 17,000 different items to make latex? Would you have submitted a manuscript over 700 times to get it published? Could you have believed in your own material that much? Herman Melville did. If he hadn't submitted his manuscript of *Moby Dick* over 700 times, we probably would not have it in our libraries today.

Sometimes we have to change our thinking, and that change may alter our vocabulary. If you have difficulty with that word "failure," then get rid of it. Don't talk about failure any more. Talk about experiences. You haven't failed 400 times. You have had 400 experiences.

Failure can be your stumbling block or your stepping stone.

"Problems" is another one of those words. "Problems" is a word that is so heavy it is like having that big, black cloud following you around like we used to see in the cartoons. Someone calls us and says, "You will not believe the problems we have lined up for you tomorrow when you get back to work." Doesn't that feel like a big, black cloud just moved in and sat down on your shoulder? Change that word. Get rid of "problems." Don't have a "problem" ever again. Have only "challenges" in your life from now on. "Challenges" are exciting. You can get your teeth into them. You can go with challenges.

When I teach at the university, I don't give "tests." Wouldn't you like to be in my class? My students love it. I do, however, give "opportunities." You have an "opportunity" to show me how much you have learned during the semester.

My students snicker and laugh about that a little bit, but it makes a difference because it takes the pressure off of them. So many people have been conditioned to get uptight and freeze when they hear the word "test." They can, however, take an "opportunity" in a more relaxed atmosphere.

Think about the word "boss." Do you ever have negative feelings when you hear the word "boss?" Do words pop into your mind like bossy, arrogant, possessive, know-it-all? I asked that question in a seminar one day, and someone immediately said, "Short, fat, and balding." I think they must have had someone specific in mind.

But isn't a good boss a good leader? Wouldn't you rather work *with* a leader than *for* a boss? Think about it.

Sometimes those words can make such a difference in the way that we approach a situation. Change the words that hold you back. Make them work for you and not against you.

3 Types of Goals

There are three types of goals: short-term, medium-term, and long-term. Short-term goals are the ones that we are going to be accomplishing today. Medium-term goals will be taking place from now to five years from now, and long-term goals will be in the next five to ten years.

Put your goals down in a stepping stone format. The one to five year goals should be stepping stones to the goals that are to be accomplished in the next ten years. The goals that are accomplished today are stepping stones to the goals that will be accomplished in one to five years.

Accomplish your goals – one step at a time.

Let's say that I want to publish a book on goal-setting within the next five years. I look at my schedule, I look at my desk, I look at my obligations, and I think there is no way that I can do this. I don't have a spot of time to sit down and write this book. But if I break my goal down into little bitty steps, then I can *make* it happen. Maybe today all I have to do is write the title for my book. Tomorrow I can begin to write an outline. The next week my goal might be to take the first topic and list 18 thoughts that need to be covered. One step at a time. It does not have to be done all at once.

It is like looking at my desk and knowing that I don't have time to clean all of it. My closet is the same way. I look at it and realize that I don't have time to clean the entire closet, but maybe I could just straighten the shoes. Maybe I could just straighten one corner of my desk. I can accomplish my goal, one step at a time.

Balancing Your Life and Your Goals

It is important when we are setting goals to balance those goals. We know we need to have a well-balanced life. We all understand that it is not nearly as easy to do as it is to say. In order to balance our lives, we need to establish goals in all areas, and that is a challenge in itself.

Look at life as though it were an old wagon wheel. We are in the center and the spokes are the significant segments of our lives. Each of those segments needs to have a specific set of goals in order for the wheel to be perfectly round. As long as it is round, it will run smoothly. If one area gets neglected, then it makes a flat spot, and the wheel will begin to jolt and bump along the road. That is usually what happens during those challenging times.

There are times in each of our lives when we have to concentrate in one area or the other for a period of time—finals at school, illness in the family, project deadlines, weight-loss programs, spiritual rededication. When those times are taking place, the wheel will necessarily be out of balance for a short period of time. That is okay. It will not be as comfortable as your normal balanced life, but we can deal with most challenges if we know that they will end.

The goal is to complete that particular segment of our lives and get it back in balance as quickly as possible. For your sake and the peace of mind of those around you, the balanced life will be the ideal place to be. Stay there as much as you can.

How do we do this? There are seven areas of your life that need to be addressed in order to have a completely balanced life. In other words, there are seven spokes on your wheel that need to be steady and strong so that they can keep the wheel running smoothly. If one is weak or broken, it requires immediate focused attention to get your life back in "round."

7 Areas of a Balanced Life

1. **Personal**
2. **Professional**
3. **Spiritual**
4. **Educational**
5. **Physical**
6. **Social**
7. **Financial**

These are in no particular order because one is no more important than the other. The interaction of the goals is what forms the smooth exterior of your wheel. When all are working well, they blend into one whole person.

Goals need to be in harmony.

Goals need to be in harmony. For example, it would be very difficult for you to write a goal saying that you want to live in the desert and the second one saying that you want to snow ski every weekend, unless, of course, you also have a goal in there to own a private jet. For most of us, living in the desert and snow skiing every weekend would not serve as compatible goals.

We need to write at least three goals for each of the seven areas of a balanced life (listed above): a short-term, a medium-term, and a long-term goal. Just as we talked about earlier, each of these goals should be stepping stones to the others. They must be written down, and they must be committed to someone who believes in you.

Sometimes, however, we just don't know what we want to do. We need to formulate a plan for our lives, and we don't know how. Here are four questions that may help you accomplish that very first goal.

How to Formulate a Plan for Your Life and Your Goals

1. What are your three most important priorities? You should be able to list your top three priorities as quickly as the snap of a finger. If not, you need to spend some time thinking about this. Your top three priorities are what keep your life stable. They are the guy wires that keep you grounded. All of your other goals are supplements to these basic ones. They must stay in place and be balanced in order for other goals to be accomplished.

For example, my top three priorities are God first, family second and job third. I work very hard at keeping those goals in balance. But as you can see, it is important for the other goals to be in place in order for these to be my guidelines. If I don't keep God first, then my personal/family goals may not be what they should be. However, if I am going to take care of my family as I should and desire to, then I have to take care of myself physically. In order for my job goals to be attained, I have to attend to my educational goals, and they, then, provide for my financial goals which go right back to my family goals, social goals, and my spiritual goals. Thus the roundness of the wheel. Does that make sense?

If you ever find that your life is just a little bit out of keel, if it is just not going quite as smoothly as you would like for it to, go back to your basic priorities. If they are not in order, things will not go well for you.

How would you live your life if you knew that you could not fail?

2. If you only had six months to live, what would you do? Would you be doing the same thing you are doing today, or would it be different? We all only have today. Yesterday is gone, tomorrow is only a dream, today is ours. When we live in the future, we miss the joys of today. When we live in the past we are dying. Today is our gift. Don't waste it. Get up every morning asking God what glorious thing He has planned for you today, and go to bed every night thanking Him for being with you through whatever you have experienced.

3. How would you be spending your time today if you could select anything that you would like to do and there was nothing in your way—no time barriers, no money barriers, no talent barriers, and no educational barriers? Sometimes we get so buried in our daily lives that we forget that dreams are free. If you do not dream, you cannot have. Without your dreams you don't know where to set your goals, and without your goals nothing intentional is going to happen. You will just be. You will never become.

4. How would you live your life if you knew that you could not fail? How would you live your life if you were not afraid to fail? What is the worst thing that could happen if you were to fail? Are you afraid that you would have to start over again? Is that so bad? You have done it more times than you choose to remember. Do you remember how many times you fell down when you were learning to walk? Do you remember how many tries it took to say your own name? Do you remember how long it took you to learn to put on your clothes or to tie your shoes?   You are good at starting over. You just choose not to remember. Just because we are "grown up" now shouldn't make that much difference. We should never lose the persistence and determination that we had as children. If we kept that in our lives throughout our lifetime, there would be no limit to what we could accomplish.

Think through these four questions very carefully. They may help you begin to develop some of the areas that you want to work on in the future. Remember, there is no disgrace in failure. The disgrace is in not trying.

Take those goals that you have established and write them down on 3-by-5 cards, put them in your Blackberry, or post them on your mirror. Read them three times a day—*out loud*. You will be amazed how quickly things will begin to happen.

What are Affirmations?

Writing goals correctly is a big part of making them happen. We need to write them in the form of affirmations. Affirmations are statements that help to reprogram the mind. Our brain has two parts: the conscious and the subconscious. The conscious brain has the ability to make choices, to decide and to analyze. The subconscious does not have these abilities. It is much like a computer. It gives out what you put in. If it is programmed negatively, it helps to produce negative results. If it is programmed positively, it will help to produce positive results.

Affirmations are the key. Take each of your goals and turn them into an affirmation. Then read them out loud as often as possible—at least three times each day. This programs your subconscious mind. It receives your affirmations—in your own voice—and knows nothing more than to begin assisting with the orders that it has just received. Good thoughts in, good thoughts out.

You will begin to notice that you will be more aware of opportunities, ideas, and people who can and are willing to help with your goals. You will notice a heightened sense of awareness of everyone and everything around you that are related to what you are doing and where you are going.

Affirmations help reprogram your brain.

Let me give you an example. When you write affirmations, they need to include three aspects. I call them the "3 P's." They stand for Positive – Present – Personal. If I want to learn to play golf, I need to write a goal like this: "I play golf very well." I know, you are saying that I can't say that because I don't play golf at all. But I can begin to program my subconscious mind to do just that.

Let's analyze this statement: "I play golf very well." Is it positive? Yes. Is it present? Yes. Is it personal? Yes. To set an effective affirmative goal, I cannot do it in a negative tone: "I can't play golf, but I would like to." That simply tells the subconscious mind that I can't play golf, and it says, "Okay, you can't play golf, so there is no need for me to help you."

I can't do it in the future or the past —"I want to play golf"— because this tells my subconscious mind that I will play golf later, so don't worry about it now.

I can't do it for anyone but me —"You play golf very well"— as I can't play golf for you, and my subconscious surely can't help you.

Remember, the subconscious gives out what it receives or is programmed with. When I say, "I play golf very well," I am telling the truth in advance, but I am also programming the subconscious to help me with whatever I need to make this happen. It will make me aware of opportunities to learn from others. It will help me notice special classes or lessons that I might not have noticed in the paper. It will help me be aware of the fitness that I need to acquire. In short, it heightens my awareness of what needs to happen to make this goal a reality.

How Do You Visualize?

Visualization is also a powerful tool in goal-setting. If you can see what you want to accomplish, it prints a visual image on your brain that will pop up more often than you think. We talked earlier in this chapter about creating an image of the house you want—in the greatest of details. Maybe you want a new car. Maybe it is a new boat or a larger paycheck. The commission check that I photocopied and changed to the figure that I wanted to see was my visualization of that goal. I carried it in my briefcase and looked at it often. The visualization reinforced my daily affirmations. I did that until the day that check came in.

Two of the greatest tragedies in life are to not set a goal and to not set a new one.

Years ago my husband decided he wanted a bass boat. He set his goal and started affirming it every time we got in the car. We all got so tired of hearing him say, "Bass boat, bass boat." But it was amazing how aware we became of bass boats as we drove around. It wasn't long until the one he had pictured was located and acquired and, I have to say, we were all very grateful and did have a lot of fun in it.

Affirmations and visualizations are important parts of goal setting. There has been a great deal of material put together on these subjects. All of our famous athletes use visualization. Listen to them talk. Listen to what they say after a golf tournament or a ball game. Listen to how they say things. Listen to Tom Watson tell you how he used to dream when he was a child that he would one day win the Master's Golf Tournament. He didn't just sort of wander out on the golf course one day and start playing fantastic golf. He spent years dreaming, visualizing, and working to make that dream come true.

Norman Vincent Peale said that there are **four basic factors for success:**

1. **Goal Setting**
2. **Positive Thinking**
3. **Visualization**
4. **Believing**

Peale emphasized that you can bring almost any situation to a successful outcome by using these four basic factors. He said that you have accomplished as much this year as you have intended to accomplish. That is a pretty strong statement. Think about it. Not having goals is a major time-waster.

It has been said that the **two greatest tragedies** in life are:

1. **To not have set a goal.**
2. **To have reached a goal and not have set a new one.**

We have discussed why having goals is so important. It is equally as important, and, yes, a tragedy, if you accomplish one goal and do not set another.

When I was a senior director with Mary Kay Cosmetics, our unit decided that we wanted to win a pink Cadillac. That required a big production for our unit and thus a big goal. Our first, or stepping-stone goal, was to build enough volume to qualify for a pink Buick. We broke the needed volume down to monthly, weekly, and daily sales quotas for each person on the team.

Once we won the pink Buick, we used that stepping stone to take us on to the pink Cadillac. The Buick was our motivator. We knew how to do it, we knew we could do it, and so we went to work.

The pink Cadillac goals were accomplished in the same bite-sized manner as were the pink Buick goals. There was one difference, however; once we won the Cadillac, we didn't have a bigger and better car ahead of us to keep the momentum going. If we quit working, we would lose that car faster than we won it.

You have to have a dangling carrot in front of you at all times to keep going. As it became evident that we were going to win the pink Cadillac, it was necessary to develop new goals that would maintain the qualifications of that car.

Once you have the momentum of goal setting going, you can't quit. If you quit, you will have to start over again at square one. It is much easier to enjoy the momentum than it is to start the engine.

Take a few minutes sometime today and write down the 20 things that you like to do more than anything else, and then beside that list write down the 20 things that you would like to have if there were no restrictions on your life. Look at those two lists. Compare them. See how they relate to each other. You may discover some of the things that could be or should be your goals or the advanced goals in your plan.

Each month, review and rewrite, if necessary, your goals. Sometimes they will need to be changed. Sometimes they will need to be expanded. Sometimes they need to be restricted. Sometimes you need to set new ones.

Set aside time every day to work on your "A" priority goals. Emphasize the results rather than the activities, and try to accomplish at least one step toward your goal every day.

Work on your "A" priority goals every day.

Some say it is better to be doing something without a plan than to be doing nothing. They forget that making a ship seaworthy and charting a course is far from doing nothing. One hour spent in effective planning is equal to three to four hours of execution time. Without a chart, you are left adrift in a sea of stress. If you don't have the time to plan for yourself, you'll end up reacting and executing the plans of someone else. Is that how you want to live? Are these the choices that you want to have, the choices that are made by someone else? If someone else is making your choices, you may end up on Friday wondering where the week went. Or, you may end up on your death bed wondering where your life went. The choice is always yours.

H.E.L.P.

Go to www.howtogetandkeepajob.com for free work pages:
Instructions for a Prosperity Thinking Chart
Goal-Setting Form

CHAPTER 6
Skill No. 3 - Assertion versus Aggression

Laughter is an instant vacation.

Milton Berle

"Could you, uh, maybe, uh, see, uh, your way around, uh, to, uh maybe, uh, giving me a raise?"

"I want a raise. I've been doing my job around here and it is time that you gave me a raise. So I want it now."

"I would like to have a raise. I feel that I have accomplished all that is required for this position and that it is appropriate for a raise consideration."

Three types of behavior, all very different, similar words but very different attitudes, and the response to each of these behaviors will also be very different.

The first one, the stuttering and stammering, is evidence of a passive behavior pattern. Probably what would happen if I walked into a boss' office and said something like that is they would not only kick me out but also give me three more projects on the way.

The second response is what is known as aggressive behavior. That is a good way to get fired. When you tell your boss that they "have" to give you a raise, you will most likely be shown the door.

The third response is known as assertive behavior. It is the most powerful behavior pattern that we have available to us.

There are four kinds of behavior patterns: passive, aggressive, assertive, and passive-aggressive. Let's look at each of them a little more carefully.

A Passive Behavior Pattern

For example, let's say that I am going to a restaurant. It is about 12 o'clock and I have a meeting at 12:30. I am running very late, haven't had any breakfast, and I really need to get something to eat before this upcoming long meeting.

I walk into a very crowded restaurant, look around, and try to find a place I can quickly sit down and eat. The waiter walks past me. The second time he walks past me, I try to catch his attention, but I don't succeed in doing so. He walks past me three more times without noticing me, and I finally look at my watch and notice that if I don't leave right now, I am going to be late to the meeting. So, I get up, walk back to my office, and probably say to myself; "What is wrong with you? Can't you speak up for yourself? Why do you let people walk on you like that? You didn't have any breakfast and now you haven't had any lunch. What are you going to do, just feel miserable all afternoon? What *is* wrong with you? You n*ever* stand up for yourself!"

I have just exhibited what is known as passive behavior. Did anyone win in this situation? Actually, the waiter won. No one bothered him. In passive behavior, someone always loses. This time it was me. Passive behavior is known as a win-lose behavior.

Defining Aggressive Behavior

Let's go back to the restaurant. It is 12 o'clock, and I have an important meeting at 12:30. I am very anxious to get something to eat and get back to this meeting. I walk into the restaurant and notice that it is very crowded. I look around and finally push my way into a seating area. The waiter passes by me once, but the second time he walks in my direction, I grab his arm and say, "Look fellow, I'm a very important person, I have a meeting in 20 minutes, and I have to eat now. You got it?"

I may or may not get to eat. In fact, it might not be a good idea to eat what is served. It might not be safe. What I have just done is exhibit aggressive behavior, and in this type of behavior, no one wins. Aggressive behavior is a lose-lose behavior pattern. He felt walked on, and I will probably go back to my office and say to myself, "What is wrong with you? He was just trying to do his job. Why couldn't you be nice? It wasn't necessary to be ugly. You don't always have to get your way just when you want it. He was not picking on you. Why can't you be nice to people?"

Aggressive people pay for their aggression – almost every time.

I know that you are thinking about aggressive people who never seem to feel sorry for what they do or say. Not all aggressive people realize that this is a lose-lose behavior pattern, and therein lies the challenge. But they do pay for their aggression – almost every time. They pay for it in ways that you may never see. It may be through stress, ulcers, insomnia, or other stress-related disorders, but they do pay.

Recognizing Positive Assertive Behavior

Let's go to the restaurant one more time. I walk into the restaurant. It is 12 o'clock. I have an important meeting at 12:30 and am in quite a hurry to eat and get back to the office. The restaurant is very crowded, but I finally find a place to sit and, anxious as I am, the waiter walks past me the first time. The second time he walks past me, however, I gently touch his arm and say, "I realize you are busy. I need to eat."

Now who is going to win? That is right—everyone.

Assertive behavior is the only opportunity for everyone to win. It does not guarantee that everyone will win, but it is the only opportunity that you are going to have for a win-win situation. The neat thing about assertive behavior is that you can look back on something that happened maybe five years ago and if you dealt with it assertively, even if you did not win, you are still going to feel good about the manner in which you handled the situation. It is the most powerful communication tool that we have available to us in both personal and professional situations.

Assertive behavior is the only opportunity for everyone to win.

What Does Passive-Aggressive Behavior Look Like?

Let's look at passive-aggressive behavior. Then we will come back and discuss techniques for an effective assertive behavior pattern.

I have a daughter who, when she was growing up, had the cleanest closet in all of Oklahoma. Her closet was immaculate. The reason why her closet was always so clean was because there was never anything in it. All of her clothes were on the floor around her bed. I frequently looked at her room and wondered how she was ever going to get out of it alive. However, every morning, she would appear for breakfast with beautifully clean, styled hair, neat clothes, and perfect makeup. I have no idea how that ever happened.

As you can imagine, as she was growing up, that room was a source of contention between my daughter and me. One particular weekend she and I had another confrontation over her room, and she promised me that she would clean it up. Monday morning I looked down the hall, and there was that room, ready to be declared a disaster area. I knew that I should say something. But if I said anything, we would probably have a fight. If we had a fight, she would probably be late to school. If she was late to school, she would miss some classes. I don't want her to miss any classes. I don't want her to be late for school and, frankly, I don't feel like having a fight with her this morning, so I let her go on to school, and I don't say anything about her room. I just stuff it all down inside.

About 10 o'clock my husband calls me and says, "Honey, I need for you to run some errands for me today." Now my husband knows that when I am at home between lecture schedules, my schedule is very tight. I barely have time to run my own errands, much less his. But sometimes he needs to feel a little special, and sometimes he forgets about how tight my schedule is. I want him to feel important, and I don't want him to feel like my work is so important that I don't have time for him and the family, so I don't say anything to him about my busy day. I cancel my appointments, I run his errands, and I stuff it down inside.

I have a luncheon today with a friend with whom I do a lot of business. It is very important that I see her because I am leaving town again in a couple of days, and we have some important issues to address. She calls me about 10 minutes until 12 and says "something has come up," and she can't have lunch today. I really need to talk with her, but I don't want to upset her, and I don't want her to be unhappy with me, and I don't want to take a chance on losing her business, so, I don't say anything to her. I let her cancel the luncheon, and I just stuff it down inside.

I'm fixing a quick dinner for the family this evening because I am teaching at the university tonight, and my youngest daughter comes home with an unexpected guest. I don't have enough food fixed for an unexpected guest, but I don't want to embarrass the guest, I don't want to upset my daughter, I don't want to have a fight with anybody, and I don't want anybody to be unhappy, so, I don't say anything to anybody. I just spread the food out a little thinner, we go ahead and have dinner, and I stuff it down inside.

When I get to the university tonight, the dean catches me as I am walking to my office. He says, "Oh, Donna, I am so glad I caught you. Dr. Jones is ill, and I told him that I was sure that you would not mind covering for him since his class meets in the period between your two classes tonight." I don't want to teach for Dr. Jones tonight. I need to go to my office. I have paperwork to do. But I don't want the dean to be unhappy with me, I don't want him to think that I am not cooperative and that I am not helpful, and I want people to know that I will fill in for them when they need it because I know that they will do that for me, so, I don't say anything. I teach the extra class, and I stuff it down inside.

Now it is about 10 o'clock, and I start home. I suddenly realize that we don't have any milk for breakfast, so I stop by the local quick stop. Just as I drive up, the young man who runs the store is locking the front door. You know what happened to him.

I came flying out of that car screaming and hollering, "You can't close that store! It is 30 seconds until 10 o'clock, and if I don't get some milk my family won't have any breakfast. I have to get in there right now. You can't close the door! You can't do this to me!" I go on and on and on. What happened?

We all have this little gunny sack down inside, and sometimes we stuff and stuff and stuff, and when it gets full, it explodes, and it may be to the person who just barely touched the back of your leg with the grocery cart in the grocery store. That is passive-aggressive behavior.

When our little "gunny sacks" get full, they will explode!

Anne's been working a lot of overtime. She hasn't been assertive enough to tell her boss that she didn't want to work this overtime or didn't feel that she could.

So, little things begin to happen. Anne's husband says he needs some papers run off and asks her if she could find a copy machine somewhere today. She tells him that it is no problem; she will just run them off at the office.

Her daughter needs some pencils for school and asks Anne if she will get some for her that day. No problem, there are lots of pencils at the office.

Anne begins to come in late for work. She begins to take a little longer for breaks and lunch. She begins to make more personal phone calls than she has in the past. What is happening here? Anne is saying, "They owe it to me." This is passive-aggressive behavior.

We are going down the hall to our staff meeting. We have great staff meetings. We have a great staff. We all work well together and have an excellent communication level. However, today, as we are walking down the hall, Tom is not saying anything. Tom usually interacts with all of us, but today he is not saying anything. We go into the meeting, sit down, and begin working on the agenda. Things are moving along quite smoothly, except Tom is not saying anything. Ten, fifteen, twenty minutes into the agenda have now passed, and Tom is still not saying anything. Who has taken control of the meeting? You bet. Tom has. Maybe Tom learned a long time ago, maybe even when he was a child, that if he got very quiet, he could take control of a situation. That is passive-aggressive behavior.

8 Assertive Behavior Techniques

1. Use the "I" language. A lot of us were programmed when we were children that using the "I" language was a self-centered or egotistical thing to do, and now I am telling you to use it. When you do so, you are taking responsibility for your own emotions. Your emotions belong to you. They do not belong to anyone else.

As mature, responsible adults, we are totally and completely responsible for our own emotions. No one can make us happy unless we choose to let them make us happy. No one can make us angry unless we choose to let them make us angry. I cannot go up to you and say, "You make me so angry." That is not fair. In the first place, you cannot make me angry unless I allow it. It doesn't mean that I cannot become angry, and it doesn't mean that I can't express that emotion. It just means that I need to accept responsibility for it. It is much more accurate to say, "I am so angry." Does that sound different? Does it feel different? Absolutely. I am still expressing my emotions, but I am not dumping on you when I use the "I" language.

2. Use short responses. If I need to talk with you about something, I am much more assertive if I mention it to you in one, two or three short sentences rather than going on and on about it. For example, I might come up to you and say, "There is something we need to talk about. Is this a good time?" That is an assertive approach and is much more effective than if I said, "There is something we need to talk about. Is this a good time? I mean, I tried to talk to you about it last week, but you didn't want to talk about it, and I did the same thing a month ago, but you didn't want to talk about it then either and, oh well, forget about it. We will do it some other time. I'm sorry."

What you can't see, in addition to this long response, is the body language. Probably what I would have done with that long response is to begin very assertively and then gradually add more rapid hand and body movements, as I moved further and further away from you. Certainly my eyes would have moved away from you as I said, "I'm sorry." "I'm sorry" is a strong sign of passive behavior. Of course, when we are wrong, we want to say, "I'm sorry," to someone, but people who are passive have a tendency to say, "I'm sorry," all day long.

As a passive person, I would say such things as, "You dropped your pencil, I'm sorry." "You walked into the doorway, I'm sorry." "You stubbed your toe, I'm sorry." I have nothing to do with you stubbing your toe or walking into the doorway or dropping your pencil. There was no reason for me to be sorry.

Numbers 3, 4, and 5 are closely related:

3. Slow down.

4. Deepen your voice.

5. Be aware of your tone of voice.

Have you ever noticed that when you are angry, the tone of your voice has a tendency to get higher and higher? In addition, when you get very angry, you will tend to also talk much more rapidly, sometimes so rapidly that no one can understand you.

The ability to keep your conversation in a controlled tone and pace is a sign of an assertive personality. Consciously deepening your voice will add to that control. When we are communicating with someone, only seven percent of what we are communicating comes from our choice of words. Thirty-eight percent comes from our tone of voice, and 55% comes from nonverbal communication. (This is discussed more extensively in Chapter 9.)

Using the "I" language prevents dumping.

6. Use positive nonverbal communication. A passive person has a tendency to slump. They may drop their shoulders, stick their hands in their pockets, keep their head down, and certainly avoid eye contact.

The aggressive person is more likely to stand with their feet slightly apart, maybe the hands on the hips, and give the appearance of a very powerful person. They sometimes will take their glasses off and throw them on the table in an exhibition of power and control. They have been known to hit the table. If you are a historian, you will remember in 1960 when Khrushchev was speaking to the United Nations, it appeared that he removed his shoe and beat the table. Interestingly enough, they now tell us that if you look carefully at the tapes, you will discover that he never took off his shoe. In actuality, the shoe he hit the table with came from the inside of his briefcase. It was an intentional act of aggression.

We also find that aggressive people have a tendency to glare. They say that there are only three types of people who glare: aggressive people, mothers, and lovers. Have you ever been in a restaurant and watched two lovers as they were glaring at each other's eyes? It makes you wonder how they are ever going to find their mouths. Of course, maybe they don't care.

Assertive stances are very powerful, but powerful in a comfortable sort of way. It gives off an "I feel good about myself" appearance. It is not egotistical, it is just self-confidence. Their feet are slightly separated so that they are standing firmly on both feet. Their shoulders are straight and natural, and it is obvious from the way they stand that they feel good about themselves. They will look you in the eye, but they do not glare.

Notice, I said that they will look you in "the" eye, not in your "eyes." It is impossible to look into both eyes of another person. Your eyes do not work that way. Your eyes must meet at a focal point in order to function properly. It is therefore impossible for both of your eyes to look at both of their eyes.

Choose one eye or the other to concentrate on. If you are shaking hands, it is better to look at their right eye because that follows the line of your arms, as you always shake hands with your right hands.

Remember, concentrating on one eye can also create a hypnotic affect. If you focus on one eye, it is difficult for that person to look away from you, and you have a much better opportunity of keeping their attention while you are trying to share with them.

7. **Consider everyone's feelings, thoughts, ideas, and opinions.** This is the key to assertive behavior. Remember in the restaurant scenario when I talked with the waiter, I said, "I realize you are busy. I need to eat." I took his thoughts, feelings, ideas, and opinions into consideration, but I also took mine into consideration. When I recognize that you have thoughts, ideas, feelings, and opinions and that you have a right to have them, I am paying you a compliment, and that is an assertive behavior pattern. I do not have to agree with those thoughts, ideas, feelings, and opinions, but I do need to respect them. I may say to you, "John, you have said thus and such. I happen to disagree." That is an assertive behavior.

"But" and "however" are known as reversal words.

8. **Avoid the use of "but" or "however."** "But" and "however" are known as reversal words. They negate any comment that is made prior to the time that they are used. If someone comes up to you and says, "That is an excellent report you put together, but…" What does that say to you? If you get a performance evaluation, and your boss says to you, "I'm considering you for a raise with our organization, however…" Do you really think you are going to get a raise?

Negating words are words that wipe out whatever was said in the past. Once again, remember what I said to the waiter. "I realize you are busy." Period. "I need to eat." Period. When you are using assertive behavior, you take the other person's thoughts, feelings, ideas, and opinions into consideration first, and then you state your own thoughts, feelings, ideas, or opinions. They are two separate and distinct statements. They can be connected by the word "and," or they can become two separate statements which both end in a period. If I had said to the waiter, "I realize you are busy 'but' I need to eat," then I would have wiped out any consideration that I had given to him in the first statement.

A Personal Challenge

Let me give you a challenge as you're thinking about these assertive behavior patterns. Record the conversations in your office or the area where you happen to work or spend most of your time, maybe your kitchen or maybe in your car. Record the conversations where you interact with people the most for a period of 24 hours. See what kind of behavior patterns you are exhibiting. You'll be able to learn a lot just from the tone of your voice. We can use the same words, and by simply changing the tone of our voice, we can change our behavior patterns.

If you have never had any assertiveness behavior training, I sincerely recommend that you take any opportunity you have to get some. Assertiveness is another way that we can effectively deal with stress in our lives because it is another way that we feel in control and comfortable with our behaviors. It is a way to feel good about ourselves. It is an enhancement of our self-esteem.

You can get additional training through books, CDs, and seminars. Remember one thing: you can read all the books in the world or listen to all the CDs in the world or attend all the available seminars, but if you don't put the ideas into practice, they won't work. It is like me giving you all the material available in the entire world on tennis, but if you never pick up a tennis racket, you still can't play tennis.

Also be aware that you will not automatically become good at assertive behavior just because you are working at it. It is just simply not going to work every time, and that is okay. Don't be impatient. Keep trying. It will work more frequently if you keep trying, but if you goof up once in a while, it is okay. I work with assertiveness behavior patterns almost every day. I have used them in seminars. I have taught seminars on assertiveness training. I have used it with people in public, I have used it with my family, and I still goof up once in a while. It just happens.

Not long ago, I was getting ready to take a flight out of Oklahoma City. It happened to be a Sunday afternoon, and usually my flight schedules are very, very tight. That particular afternoon, I had a very loose schedule, and when I walked up to the counter to check in, the ticket agent said, "Would you consider taking a free ticket anywhere you want to go in exchange for taking a later flight today since our flight is overbooked?" Since my schedule was pretty loose that day, I thought, why not? I can do that today. Normally I could not. So, I said, "Yes, I'll do that," and they put my name down at the top of the list. I saw them write it down. We got on the plane, and they came out and called me and three men off the plane. At the very last minute, they came to us and said, "Oh, by the way we only need for three of you to stay off the plane. We thought we needed four but were mistaken, so one of you needs to go ahead and get back on the plane." These three gracious men quickly stood up, looked at me, and said, "You go ahead and get on the plane."

What really made me angry was that I did! Then it occurred to me that these men were not being nice to me, they just simply wanted that free ticket, and I had just given it to them. I was so angry with myself that I sat there the entire flight and figured out what I should have said.

I have this down pat. It was so easy. All I needed to say was, "I realize that you gentlemen would like to have a free ticket. My name happens to have been first on the list. One of you needs to make a decision to get on that plane."

Now every time I get ready to go to the airport, my husband will say to me, "Honey, is your flight overbooked today?" I say, "Honey, I don't really know." Then he will say, "If it is, do you know what to say?"

It doesn't work every time. It is, however, worth the effort because assertiveness behavior is the most powerful tool that you can use. I think you will find it a very successful way to be in control of your life and help you stand out in the crowd.

H.E.L.P.

Go to www.howtogetandkeepajob.com for free work pages:
Recording form for self evaluation

Notes

CHAPTER 7
Skill No. 4 - Creative Communication Skills

Never be afraid to try something new. Remember,
amateurs built the ark. Professionals built the Titanic.

Author unknown

CCS Means "Caring"

"That is why he didn't turn the report in. He didn't even hear me request it."

"I'm going home and apologizing to my daughter. I have been trying to communicate wrong with her for 21 years."

"It is so nice to know that I am not stupid!"

These are comments made to me at seminars after we had discussed what I refer to as CCS, or Creative Communication Skills.

What Is CCS?

CCS is a technique by which we can improve both our personal and professional relationships tremendously. An essential part of communication is sending and receiving information. Unless we send information to people in the manner in which they choose to receive it, we can have a serious breakdown in that interaction.

People receive information basically three ways. They receive visually, through their eyes; aurally, through their ears; or kinesthetically, through touch. Most of us receive in all three of these ways, but we usually receive predominately in one of the three. When we recognize how people receive information, we can affect their lives more deeply and let them know that we really care.

For example, if you are going to give me directions to the airport when I am in a strange city, give me very explicit directions. I want to know which way to go out of the hotel, and whether I turn left or right at the corner. Don't tell me to get on I-10 because I probably don't know where it is. Either write down the directions for me, or give me a chance to write as you talk. Otherwise, I won't retain half the information and may never arrive at the airport. This does not mean that I am not intellectually capable. It just means I am visual.

If I happen to be an aural person, giving me the same information on the telephone or as we walked down the hall would be no problem. In fact, it was a good thing you did because if you had written me a note or memo, I might not have gotten around to reading it this month.

If you want a kinesthetic person to remember, you need to have some kind of physical contact with them like a pat on the back, a handshake, or maybe a hug, depending on the situation. This type of interaction with a kinesthetic person has the same impact as direct eye contact has with a visual person.

Let's see how this affects our personal and professional relationships.

Energizing Personal Relationships

I am a very, very visual person. Suppose my mom and a good friend both sent me funny cards last week. I will probably have those cards a year from now. I carry in my briefcase, all the time, the valentine card my husband sent me last year. On the dressing table in my bathroom are the last birthday and anniversary cards I received from him. They will remain there until my new birthday and anniversary cards arrive, at which time I will exchange them. I have kept the notes that my kids have sent me ever since they were in grade school. I keep special notes, letters, and articles from my family and friends. When someone writes me a letter of praise and recognition, I keep it – forever. I do this because I am a visual person. Those things mean a great deal to me. Now, I am not a hoarder, but I do want those special items.

My husband is a very aural person—very, very aural. He quickly picks up things through his ears. I can go and spend an hour and a half picking out a beautiful card for him. He will pick it up, read it quite carefully all the way through, and say, "Oh honey, thank you for the beautiful card," and then immediately throw it in the trash. I mean, right then, while I am standing there, he will take that card that I spent an hour and a half buying and throw it right in the trash can. Understanding CCS has prevented a lot of bad feelings because I know that he is aural and receives through his ears. He would have much preferred that I told him, "Honey, I love you," rather than for me to have bought him that card. We need to learn to show that we care by being aware of other people's needs. Just because I love the beautiful cards my husband sends me doesn't mean that he wants them in return.

Motivation in Professional Relationships

We cannot motivate another human being. However, we can persuade and influence them, and we can put them into an atmosphere in which they can become motivated. One of the most effective ways to do this is through CCS.

We cannot motivate another human being.

A man walked out of a little country church late one evening. Knowing that he wanted to get home before dark, he decided that he would not make it by going his usual route. "Perhaps," he thought, "I should take a shortcut across the graveyard attached to the little church."

As he walked out across the graveyard, he came upon an open grave, tripped, and fell in. After trying for some time to get out of the grave, he finally decided that it was just too deep and he was going to have to wait until morning so someone would hear him and come and get him out. So, he went over in the corner of the grave and sat down to get some rest.

Late that night the town drunk came wandering out across the graveyard. He came upon the open grave, tripped, and fell in. He tried and tried to get out. While he was doing so the other man was sitting over in the corner watching him. After a while he said, "You can't get out of here." But he did!

Now that is putting someone in an atmosphere where they can become motivated!

Let's say someone, either on your staff or in your personal life, has done something that deserves praise and recognition. If they are visual people, they will prefer that you write them a letter or a note. In fact, they may appreciate it so much that they may keep that letter or note forever. They may leave it on their desk to be seen frequently or post it somewhere or have it framed.

The aural person would prefer that you call them on the telephone or personally tell them how much you appreciate what they have done.

The kinesthetic person needs a pat on the back, a handshake, or a hug.

I had a man in a seminar who worked for a government agency. One of the comments he made was that if you work for the government, you never get any praise and recognition. The man sitting next to him immediately turned and said, "What do you mean? You have a whole bottom drawer in your desk that is full of letters of praise and recognition. You get more recognition than anyone I know." To which the original man commented, "Oh, that doesn't count." What does that tell you about him? He either needed for someone to come by and talk with him or give him a pat on the back or a good handshake. Those letters meant virtually nothing to him.

When I am on a seminar tour, I generally receive five or six hundred evaluations during any one week. Most of you receive evaluations once or twice a year. I get five or six hundred a week. They all count, just like yours do. At the end of a seminar, I will stand at the door giving out certificates of completion, and people will say special things like, "That was a great seminar; "or "You really touched my life." Of course, I love the comments, but what do I key in on? Those written evaluations. When I get to my hotel at night, I read those evaluations, carefully, one at a time. Why? Because I am visual.

Delegation in Professional Relationships

J.C. Penney said that if you want to kill executives, do not teach them how or when or to whom to delegate. Delegating is another way we communicate ideas to people, both personally and professionally. We tell people what we want them to do, how we want them to do it, and when we want it done. When we delegate to people in the manner in which they prefer to receive information, the action is much more likely to take place.

If you want to kill executives, do not teach them how or when or to whom to delegate.

During a seminar we were discussing the difference in how we should delegate to people who are visual, aural, and kinesthetic. A female executive suddenly said, "So that's why he didn't turn in the report. He didn't even know I requested it." I asked for an explanation, and she said that a couple of weeks before, in a staff meeting, she verbally requested that certain information be compiled and turned in at the next staff meeting. She went on to say that she never got around to putting the request into written form. Three of the men turned in the report, and one acted as though he had never heard about it. She suddenly exclaimed, "He's visual! He really didn't remember my asking for it." This is very possibly the answer to her dilemma.

Let's look at another example. You and I are walking down the hall, and you give me a list of nine items that you want done. If I am an aural person, that list will be no problem. Being a visual person, however, I will probably remember the first two or three and maybe the last item on the list, but the middle items will get lost somewhere along the way. Does this mean that I am stupid? Of course not. It has nothing to do with my intellectual ability. It just means I receive differently. Knowing that I am a visual person, you will rarely ever see me without a pad and a pencil. If we are walking down the hall and you are giving me a list of things to do, I will be jotting them down. If I am on the telephone, I will be taking notes. I know that I need the visual reminders.

When my husband and I are on a trip and we stop to ask for directions, unless I write it down, the directions will mean nothing to me. Robert, on the other hand, will just say, "Yes, yes, I understand," and drive directly to wherever we want to go.

Being different is okay.

Someone excitedly raised their hand in a seminar and said, "It is so wonderful to know that I am not stupid or that I am not losing it all. I am just visual!" She continued, "All this time I thought there was something wrong with me because I couldn't remember things like some of my friends and co-workers do."

Negative self-talk is an easy trap to fall into, and when we don't understand what is happening to us, it is easier than ever. Zig Ziglar says we live in a "Stinkin' Thinkin'" world. It has to be our conscious choice every day to live in a positive self-talk world. Maybe you need to stop right now and tell yourself how special you are and recognize what great talents and abilities you do have. Being different is okay.

How Do You Receive Information?

How do you know whether a person is visual, aural, or kinesthetic? Listen to what they say. Or, ask them, "How do you feel about…?" whatever it happens to be. If you are talking to me, I will probably say, "That *looks* good to me," or "I like the way that *looks*," or "I *see* what you mean." Let's say that Jean happens to be aural. What will she say? "I like how that *sounds*;" "Oh yes, I *hear* you," "*Rings* a bell with me." What is a kinesthetic person going to say? "*Feels* good to me," "I am *comfortable* with that." Listen to how people talk to you because they are telling you how they prefer to receive information.

I have one daughter who is very, very visual. If I tried to talk with her about something I wanted done, we almost always ended up in a fight. It was like a ritual. But when I wrote her a note and put it on her bed or on her mirror, things just seemed to happen. There was no discussion and no argument. Everything was just fine.

I have another daughter who is very, very aural. If I wrote her a note and put it on her bed or on her mirror, she might not read it for six months. She only checked her mail about every six months. The year she was a junior in college, she spent the summer at home. We had two telephones in our home—a personal line and a business line. They both had call-waiting, so that made a total of four lines.

When I was on the road, I called home every night. But there were nights that summer when I would call home and could not get through. Why? Because she would have all four lines tied up at the same time. When she was at home, you didn't hear the telephone ringing constantly. It usually rang one time on each line in the evening, and that was all. The rest of the calls came in on call-waiting, for hours and hours and hours. This was before cell phones and e-mail, and I sometimes felt I needed to send my husband a telegram so that he would know that I had arrived safely!

Our daughter was an excellent student. She would just go to class and soak up all the information right through her ears. She picked up everything through her ears.

Had the girls been kinesthetic, they would have been okay when I wrote them a note or told them what I wanted done, but they would also have wanted a hug.

I was telling this story in one of my seminars, and at the end, a woman came up to me almost in tears. She said, "I'm going home and apologize to my daughter. Because of what you said today, I have suddenly realized that I have been trying to communicate wrong with her for 21 years. You have really made a difference in our lives."

Not understanding how we receive communication can be a source of great misunderstanding. Think how many times my feelings would have been hurt over the years if I hadn't understood why my husband throws all my cards away. Has this happened to you, too?

Not understanding how we receive communication can be a source of great misunderstanding.

What are you? Are you a visual person? Do you want me to write you a note to say thank you? Are you a keeper? Or are you aural? Are you a person who never needs to write anything down? Are you the one who controls the TV channel selector? Or, are you kinesthetic? Are you the hugger? There are usually fewer people who are kinesthetic than there are people who are visual or aural, but they are just as important.

Even though we generally prefer to receive in one of the three manners, we normally continue to receive visually, aurally, and kinesthetically. Sure I love to have my husband give me a hug or tell me he loves me, but what I really key in on are those notes he writes and cards he sends me. I read them over and over again because I am predominately visual. (As he finished proofreading this chapter, my husband wrote me the following note, "I like it. I love you." Do you think I am going to throw that away?)

How to Apply CCS

When I gave a seminar, I had no way of knowing how each of the several hundred people in the room would be receiving information. So I had to do a variety of things to reach them. I would start the day by trying to shake hands with each of them. Then I would do a verbal seminar which was backed up with visuals like overheads and printed workbooks for them to follow along. During the day, I made as much physical and one-on-one contact with the participants as I could. At the end of the seminar, I once again made contact with each individual at the door as they left. I got excellent ratings, and I think it had a lot to do with the fact that I was able to communicate information to almost every individual in the manner in which they preferred to receive it.

Do you want to stand out in the crowd? Then remember that most of us just want someone to care about us. Through CCS we can begin to show people that we really do care enough to praise, recognize, and delegate to them in the way they receive best. After all, caring is what life is all about.

H.E.L.P.

Go to www.howtogetandkeepajob.com for free work pages:
Recording sheet for personal and professional references

Notes

CHAPTER 8
Skill No. 5 -Time Management

I recommend you take care of the minutes,
for the hours will take care of themselves.

Chesterfield

How Do You Instill Confidence in Yourself?

Why is it that the busiest people get everything done while the rest of us drown in half-finished projects, despairing over all those things we meant to do, but didn't? Why do so many of us have trouble getting things done?

You get 86,400 seconds every day.
You use them, or you lose them.
Your choice.

4 Reasons Why We Don't Get Things Done

1. **We fail to set priorities.**

2. **We procrastinate.**

3. **We bite off more than we can chew.**

4. **We try to do everything perfectly.**

Do you ever get the feeling that you spend half of your time waiting for a light to change? Actually, most of us spend only 6 months of our lives idling at red lights, even it if seems longer. Opening junk mail takes up to 8 months of our time. Searching for misplaced items gobbles up 1 year (until you get older, and then it is more). Two years are wasted trying to return phone calls to people who aren't in.

(Voice mail and e-mail help a lot.) House work fills up 4 years, and most of us wait in lines for 5 years of our life. Eating takes up 6 years, and 7 years are spent in the bathroom. This does not account for having teenagers in the house.

If someone deposited $86,400 into your bank account every morning with the stipulation that you can have it every single day if you use it in its entirety and do not waste any of it, what would you do? That is exactly what happens every time you have a new day. You have 86,400 seconds to spend. They belong to you entirely and completely. They are yours to use whatever way you choose. You can use them or lose them. It is your choice.

We want to learn how to walk through life rather than run through it. We want time to be peaceful and not full of pressure. That is how we want to be seen by the people with whom we are working.

Time is money in a company. If you waste their time, you are wasting their money, the money they have with which to employ you. Is it, therefore, important to be on time? Is it important to make and keep an accurate schedule for appointments? Is it worth the effort to never miss a deadline?

We have a tendency to say, "If I had as much time as Tom over there, you wouldn't believe what I could get done. I would get so much more done every day if I had even half as much time as he does."

Does Tom have more time than you do? Absolutely not. It is just the way he manages it.

To be a little more accurate, it isn't exactly that he "manages" his time. The term "time management" is a misnomer. You cannot manage time. It is a universal gift and not a management technique. What you need to do is to save it. But can you do that? Can you go to lunch, spend only a half hour, put the other half hour in a baggie, and take it home for tonight? That would be very nice. However, it just won't work, and since we cannot "save" or "manage" time, what do we have to learn to manage? You've got it. We have to learn to manage ourselves.

Is this important? Only if you want to be the one to stand out in the crowd and have the opportunity to keep your job or get a promotion. Punctuality, accuracy, dependability, deadlines, and learning to respect the time of not only yourself but of your bosses and your customers/clients are what will make the difference.

We must learn to manage ourselves, so that we use time in an effective manner. Feeling guilty about the loss of it is a total waste of time. Feeling guilty is not going to bring it back, so don't worry about it. Move on and learn from the experience.

Learn that managing ourselves, and thus our time, is directly related to our goal setting and to our priorities. In other words, it has a direct relationship to all the things that we feel are important in our life and work. It helps to prevent procrastination so that we can learn to do the most challenging and undesirable task first in the day and not have to spend the entire day being miserable thinking about it.

In Chapter 11, we talk about doing a time management study. I hope you make time to do it. If so, you will become aware of where you spend your time, and your time wasters should be very apparent.

As you look at that chart, ask yourself these four questions: What were your most significant accomplishments? How many activities were enjoyable to you? How often were you bored or unhappy? If you continue as you have in the past week, where will you be in five years?

We don't plan to fail, we fail to plan.

Goals can save you time. In Chapter 5, we talked extensively about goals and goal-setting. Goals are a very important part of time management. They are our plans. We don't plan to fail, we fail to plan and that is what makes the difference.

7 Basic Goals for Time Management

1. **Planning Efficiently**

2. **Combining Activities**

3. **Eliminating the Non-essentials**

4. **Processing Telephone Calls**

5. **Controlling Meetings**

6. **Dealing with Correspondence**

7. **Learning Delegation**

Let's look at each of these a little more carefully.

1. Planning Efficiently

No matter how busy you are, you must plan your day. Use your lunch hour. Instead of just sitting around drinking coffee and reading the paper, use it for planning, running errands, having lunch with your children, studying, relaxing, exercising. In other words, **make lunch time work for you**.

Use your travel time. If you travel in a car, listen to motivational, educational, or spiritual material. Make phone calls, if you have a hands-free phone and are not required to drive in a great deal of traffic. If you do, then please, for the sake of yourself and the others around you, concentrate on your driving. Listening even when you are concentrating on driving is a much safer activity because you will absorb a great deal of the information through your subconscious mind and can use your conscious mind for driving safely. If someone else is driving, read, write, plan, and organize so that when you arrive at the office or work site, you are ready to go to work and not just ready to start your day. These techniques will help you meet deadlines head on.

We have talked a lot about standing out in the crowd. This is one of the ways that you can do that: never miss a deadline. Whether the deadline is planning and presenting a project, attending a meeting, or meeting with a customer/client, having a reputation for always being on schedule will definitely set you apart from the crowd.

Parkinson's Law says that anything will take the amount of time that is allotted for it. Set a schedule when you begin any type of project. Get a timer and use it to help control the time. I use one when I clean, and I use one when I work in my office. The best timer is one that ticks out loud so that you become aware that time is moving on.

Let's say you want to clean a room in your home or straighten your garage, but you know that you do not have time to get it all done, so the normal tendency is to just do nothing. Use a timer. Determine the amount of time that you do have to work on your project and set the timer. This sets a goal. Go to work and when the timer goes off – quit! You may not have completed the job, but at least you have done part of it, and you have completed your goal. You see, your goal was not to complete the garage; it was to work for X amount of time, and you successfully did that. You should have a great sense of accomplishment. Congratulations!

I do this in my office on a regular basis. When I traveled full-time on the lecture circuit, it was difficult to get to my office and catch up. Frequently I would be out of town for a week or two at a stretch, and the mail would be sky high when I got back to the office. My first reaction would be that there was no way I could get through all of this and that there was no use in trying. When I began to use the timer, it made all the difference in the world. I would set it for an hour or 30 minutes or whatever time I had available and go to work. The tick, tick, ticking kept me at it, and when the bell chimed, I knew that I could quit and feel good about my accomplishments.

2. Combining Activities

Planning can also be accomplished through combining your activities. Listening to motivational, educational, or spiritual CDs while you are getting ready or driving is an example of combining your activities. Making phone calls with a headset or ear plug so that you can be working in the kitchen, cleaning the garage, or straightening your office at the same time are also good examples of combining activities. Using your cell phone or Blackberry in the office provides you with the opportunity to talk with customers/clients on the way to meetings or planning sessions. You can also obtain needed information without having to return to your office.

"Make" time for the special people in your world.

Don't forget your personal life. If you are truly going to become a balanced person and, thus, much more effective in all areas of your life, learn to combine your family activities as well. My husband I have very busy schedules. It is easy to let time get away without spending it together unless we actually "make" time for each other.

My husband is an avid golfer. I don't play, but I do walk or ride with him on occasion when he is playing. That way I get to enjoy some beautiful scenery, peaceful atmosphere, and wonderful time with him.

Be creative. Find things that you are both interested in. Several of our friends antique together or exercise together. Study a particular subject that you both find interesting. You can study independently and then share your findings over a quiet dinner or even on the phone when you are traveling.

Another effective planning tool is to **set your clocks 5 minutes ahead**…all of your clocks, if possible: alarm, office, watch, car, computer, iphone. That way you are always ahead of schedule, and if an emergency happens, you are not as likely to be late. If they are all set at the same time, you will eventually forget which ones are reset, and it will become a natural way of life.

3. Eliminating the Non-Essentials

The Perito Rule is called the 80/20 rule. It says that 80% of our success depends on 20% of our activities. In other words, we spend too much time on low-priority items. We must learn to **distinguish between what is urgent and what is important**.

An important activity is one that relates to your objectives, while an urgent activity is one that must be attended to **now**. Learning how to differentiate between them can help you react and respond more effectively to daily demands and crisis. It will provide a means of keeping your projects in proper perspective and order.

Consider how much time you spend watching TV. Is this the amount that you want to spend doing this activity? Is that your manner of relaxing? Could your relaxation time be more effectively spent by reading or walking? Is your TV time a non-essential in your life or is it a priority? It is something that each of us has to make a decision about. When I am traveling or on a work schedule, I rarely watch TV. It is a non-essential. However, when my husband and I have an evening together, we can enjoy a favorite program or a movie on the TV and share that time. Then it has become a priority.

4. Processing Telephone Calls

Telephone calls are the same way. Caller ID, call waiting, and e-mailing have made it possible to prevent becoming distracted from a priority by a non-essential phone call. When the priority is handled, the calls and/or e-mails can be taken care of in a more comfortable atmosphere.

If you want to feel good about yourself and project that to others, remember that you, not someone else and not some "thing," are in charge of your life. Cell phones, e-mails, text messages, and instant messages can all become a controlling factor if you allow them to. When you are at work and messages are coming to you that are work-related and urgent, then you may have to deal with them at the moment. If they are not urgent, let them collect until you have a moment to check them. At home, it is different. These items are yours, and they should not control your life. You pay for them, and you can choose to answer or let it go. Never forget the respect that your family deserves.

Calls and messages at work not only interrupt productive time but take a great deal of unnecessary time. Fortunately, e-mails and text messages have partially eliminated the long phone calls that tend to drift on to unrelated subjects. However, we still get calls, and if you find that you are spending more time than you can afford to give to that area of your professional life, limit your business calls to three minutes. Most business calls can be taken care of in that amount of time unless it is something extremely complicated.

Bunching phone calls is a very effective way to control your time.

Bunching phone calls is a very effective way to control your time. Let your phone and/or staff collect your calls and leave a message that all calls will be returned between 4 and 5 PM (or whenever you choose) and that if it is more urgent and cannot wait until that time, to please call back. The urgent message signal in our family has always been that if we need someone immediately, we call twice in succession and hang up. When that number pops up twice in a row in a very short time, it means to call me now.

I know one female executive who returns all of her calls between 11:40 and 12:00 and 4:40 and 5:00. She says it is amazing how much business you take care of when everyone is trying to go to lunch and when they are trying to go home. All of the niceties are done away with, and business is taken care of strictly as business. This is something that you might want to consider for yourself.

Remember, a collection of these little things is what accumulates into the overall picture of someone who should be considered for a promotion and more responsibility.

5. Controlling Meetings

Another challenge is meetings. If you are responsible for the meeting, be sure that there is an agenda out 48 hours prior to the meeting so that everyone has an opportunity to prepare the material that they want to present. You need a time schedule on the agenda so that everyone is aware that you are going to discuss the plant in Peoria, Illinois, for only 10 minutes. This gives you, as the leader or the chairman of that meeting, an opportunity to stay in control because you can simply say, "Kelsey, please wind this up. We only allowed 10 minutes for the plant in Peoria, Illinois, this morning and we're running out of time. If we need to discuss this issue further, we'll need to put it on our next agenda or set up a special meeting for that purpose." The time element on the agenda is also a reminder that the meeting will start on time, end on time, and that if you are scheduled to present a topic, it needs to be condensed to be presented within the specified time limit.

Another way to control meetings is to go to someone else's office instead of allowing them to come to yours. When you are in their office, you control the time because you can get up and walk out. If they are in your office, sometimes it is not quite as easy to do. If someone comes in and tends to make themselves comfortable after the purpose of the meeting has been completed, it is appropriate to thank them for coming and walk them to the door.

6. Dealing with Correspondence

How well do you handle correspondence? Of course, the ideal situation is to handle papers only once. That is a whole lot easier to talk about than it is to do. But let me give you one challenge: This next week, every time a piece of paper passes through your hands, put a little dot in the corner and try to get rid of that piece of paper before it looks like it has the measles. Also, be aware that every time you touch that piece of paper, it costs your organization a minimum of fifty cents.

When you have a letter that needs to be answered, either shoot them an e-mail, or a text or jot an answer on the bottom of that letter and send it back. The world of business is not nearly as formal as it used to be. Efficiency has taken the place of formality in most companies.

Electronics can save you a massive amount of time. Use your Blackberry or cell phone to keep track of your schedule or to make notes to yourself of things that need to be done that day or when you return to the office. If you do not have one, then get a small recorder and carry it with you to keep notes. It is easily handled even when you are driving and have a brilliant idea pop into your head.

Each time a piece of paper passes through your hands, put a dot in the corner and try to get rid of it before it looks like it has the measles.

All of us are familiar with the Nike commercial which reminds us to "Just Do It." That is what I like to call the DIN DIN Club. It is probably the number-one most effective time management tool. Don't procrastinate. Don't put things off. **Do it now! Do it now!**

7. Learning Delegation

In Chapter 7 and again in Chapter 9, there is a section on delegation. Re-reading them will give you a good reminder of the hows and whys of delegation.

One thing that these do not cover is the importance of delegation at home. Our homes, if efficient, are run very much like a corporation. Each member of the "corporation" must do their job in order for it to run effectively. The traditional male-female roles have changed over the years. Our ancestors would never have thought about exchanging roles with each other. That is no longer true, and the fact that it is not true can make a home run much more smoothly. In other words, we, each of us, does what needs to be done, when it needs to be done. There is no such thing as "your job."

Children need responsibilities too. They need to understand the cooperation required to blend two people into a marriage relationship. We learn by seeing and hearing, which is to say, our children are not only listening to what we say to each other but also are watching our interaction as well.

It is important to be true to ourselves and our values. Never ask someone, at home or in the business world, to do something that you would not be willing to do yourself – if it were necessary. In the same line, never hesitate to ask for help when you need it. Being macho or a martyr is not a flattering personality trait. There are times when we all need help from a family member or a friend, and there is nothing wrong with asking for it. In many cases, the person you ask for help is willing and wanting to help but simply does not know what to do. Be specific and be grateful.

H.E.L.P.

Go to www.howtogetandkeepajob.com for free work pages:
Time management evaluation sheet

Notes

CHAPTER 9
Skill No. 6 - Leadership

Reasonable people equally informed seldom disagree.

Author unknown

Leadership is Required for Advancement

There are very few activities as challenging and yet as rewarding as leadership. It requires a combination of intelligence, patience, common sense, good humor, and a fundamental understanding of how to work with people.

The effective leader can multiply the value and benefits of an organization in a multitude of ways. As a leader, you are in an ideal position to contribute to the organization's increased productivity and profitability. You can influence the attitudes and performance of the workers and achieve goals that will not only be advantageous to the organization but also to the society you live in and, thus, to your personal growth.

There are many topics that need to be covered in the area of effective leadership. Only a few are being covered here. Once you acquire that position, take advantage of every opportunity to take training to improve your efficiency level and help others grow along with you. Any organization is only as strong as its weakest link, and your value will be enhanced in direct proportion to the growth of that organization.

Never be afraid of growth, yours or anyone else's. Some people are afraid that if they help their staff become proficient at their personal duties, they will no longer have a job. However, if you do not teach someone else how to do your job, you will never have an opportunity for promotion. As they grow, so do you.

In this analysis we are going to talk about how to handle challenging people, deal positively with anger, prevent mini-crises, and learn the keys to delegation—a smorgasbord of ideas which will get you started on the pathway to effective leadership. The key to getting and keeping that leadership position is to never quit learning. Make learning a lifelong process for your benefit both personally and professionally.

How to Handle "Challenging" People

Have you ever had problems dealing with a subordinate or a boss or a co-worker? If you have not, don't read this section. You don't need it. However, if that challenge has ever been part of your experience, then keep reading. You, along with the rest of us, need this information.

There are only about ten percent of the people in this world who are truly difficult. The rest of us, well, we are just different, and different is okay. Those ten percent however, will give us the same challenges day in and day out. They have just learned to cope in an interesting way. The truth is, there really are no difficult people… there are just difficult situations. Our challenge is to learn to deal with situations not only from our perspective but also from the perspective of our employee, employer, co-worker, and/or customer-client. Remember, you do not have to like people to cope with them.

There are only about 10% of the people in this world who are truly difficult. The rest of us, we are just different.

In order to be successful both on the job and in our personal lives, it is imperative that we get along with other people. Unfortunately, we all encounter difficult people at times, and it can leave us feeling frustrated and demoralized. But it doesn't have to be that way. We cannot change another human being, but we can change the way we respond to others and thus make a difference in the manner in which we interact.

Why do difficult people act the way they do? More importantly, how do we not only minimize antagonistic behavior but change forever the way we respond to those difficult people in our world? Let's find out.

We all need to feel that we are important and worthy of others' interest and consideration. If we are put down in any manner, or even in any perceived manner, this triggers our reaction to a negative encounter.

How to Be Creative when Dealing with Challenging Situations

These five steps are simple but essential if we desire to minimize the likelihood of challenging encounters:

1. **Interest:** Our favorite subject is not usually someone else. It is usually ourselves. However, if you want to minimize difficult situations, learn to be sincerely interested in others.

2. **Smile:** A number of years ago, Dan Rather replaced Walter Cronkite on the evening news. The ratings dropped drastically. It was said that the reason why was because Dan Rather didn't smile. Smiling increases the comfort level of those around you. It makes you feel a part of the group and adds to the ability of effective interaction. Watch a re-run of Oprah Winfrey sometime. She is a master at smiling at her guests and making them comfortable so that they will easily reveal probably more than they intended to.

3. **Listen:** Good listening techniques include such behaviors as eye-to-eye contact, no interruptions, repeating information for verification, and positive body language. When thinking of listening skills, I always think of the 5-year-old who took her mother by the face with both hands and said, "Mother, listen to me with your eyes."

4. **Others' feelings:** In Chapter 6, we talked about the "I" language and how important it is to assume responsibility for your thoughts, feelings, ideas, and opinions. Instead of creating more dissention by saying, "Why are you so angry?", try saying, "I can see you are angry. Can we talk about it?"

5. **MMFI:** "Make me feel important." Above the computer on my desk are a lot of signs that remind me of ideas or thoughts that I want to be a part of who I am. One of them is "Make me feel important." It is not there because I need to feel important but because I don't want to forget to treat others in the same manner in which I prefer to be treated. Sometimes we get so busy being important that we forget to make others feel important. This creates resistance because if we do not feel valued, we will react.

If we can deal with potentially challenging situations before they get out of hand, we have a better chance of forestalling any conflicts. When your senses tell you that a potentially challenging situation is at hand, ask yourself three questions:

1. **Are you looking at a challenging person or a challenging situation?**

2. **Can you accept that the only person you can change in this situation is you?**

3. **Can you develop a solution to this situation, or do you need to remove yourself from the problem?**

Once you complete the analysis and accept the fact that you do need to be involved, then you can begin to develop a potential solution. Begin by looking at the situation analytically: What are the symptoms? What is the real problem? Are there any obvious possible solutions? Can you work together on a potential solution? If a potential solution can be designed, don't just walk away and feel that all is well—check on its progress, and evaluate the level of success. If you have solved the challenge, celebrate! Buy yourself a bag of M&Ms and have a chocolate frenzy. If you have not reached a successful solution, you need to once again look at the challenge and determine if it is time to cut your losses and move on. There comes a point when you have tried hard enough. Sometimes we have to accept the fact that not everyone comes out a winner in every situation.

When you solve a challenge, celebrate! Buy yourself a bag of M&M's and have a chocolate frenzy!

Effective Anger Management

Dr. Barbara DeAngeles wrote an excellent book titled *How To Make Love All The Time.* No, it is not about sexual relationships. Sorry. It is about how to deal effectively with anger. Check it out. It may be just the one you need.

Difficult people usually know how to push your buttons. They know how to push you off balance and turn you into a war monger so that they can blame the bad situation on you instead of themselves. Don't let this happen. Be in charge of you. Deal with your emotions early. Don't let them build up and create a lot of steam. When you blow up, you not only increase your stress levels but also the stress levels of those around you. Learn how to use anger effectively. Control it. Don't let it control you. How do you do that?

5 Keys to Controlling Anger

1. Watch your body language. Fifty-five percent of how you communicate is through your body language. If you include your tone of voice, it increases to 93%. In other words, what you say is not nearly as important as how you say it.

These statistics were established in the early 1960's by Albert Mehrabian, Professor Emeritus of Psychology at UCLA. He called it the 3 V's (standing for Verbal – Vocal – Visual) or the 7-38-55 Rule.

When you are angry, make and break eye contact with the person with whom you are dealing. Do not glare and don't allow them to glare at you. We are not searching for control; we are searching for solutions. Take your nonverbal body language into a relaxed mode. Sit down and slow down the rate of speech. Don't cross your legs and swing your foot, cross your arms in a defiant or protective mode, or shake your finger. Back off, take a few slow, deep breaths, and approach the situation in a more relaxed manner.

55% of the way you communicate is through your body language.

2. **Speak directly.** Address the specific behavior that is bothering you. Use a formula such as, "When you ____, I feel ____ because ____." Avoid starting sentences with "You." This is aggressive and makes people feel as though they are being accused from the first word out of your mouth. The "I" language, which is discussed in Chapter 6, is much more effective and can rapidly lead to a good attitude for solutions discussions.

3. **Use active listening.** Repeat what the other person said to you 1) to indicate that you heard them correctly, and 2) to assure them that you really are listening. Square your shoulders and look them straight in the eye. Let them know from your body posture that what they are saying is important to you and that you do respect their thoughts, feelings, ideas, and opinions, even if you do not agree with them.

4. **If necessary, distract yourself mentally.** Sometimes we have to sit there and take it. If that happens to be the case, learn to use your mind for reflective

thinking. For example, play a mental game. Place that person on a merry-go-round or in a dance contest. Listen to only what they are saying and pay no attention to their nonverbal communication. Whatever it takes, do not allow someone else to think for you. Always investigate, analyze, theorize, and project your own ideas so that you are still your own person. This is not to say that the other person's point may not be valid and worth considering for yourself. But even if it is, let it be your decision to consider it.

5. Plan ahead. Once the discussion is over, know what you need to do to relieve the stress. Find a place where you can use up some of the pent-up energy and get the blood back in your head. In other words, chill out. Lean over and count to ten, run in place, race up the stairs, work in the yard, or do some mindless activity like working out on a rowing machine.

Good emotional health is directly related to how direct you can be to other people.

Anger is okay. It is what we sometimes do with it that is not okay. It isn't okay to direct it toward other people. We can direct it toward thoughts, ideas, and actions, but not directly to *you*. Hitting people or breaking things is never good use of anger.

Remember, this too shall pass. The only thing that will cause it to remain is if you let your anger become self-destructive. Keep it in control so that it does not create distress in your mind and body.

The Importance of Good Emotional Health

Learn to laugh at yourself. It is an extremely effective way to keep things in perspective. It never helps to blame yourself or other people when things go wrong.

Just accept it as a situation that needs to be dealt with and move on. If you, however, feel that it is a situation which you can no longer handle, please do not hesitate to get help.

Good emotional health is directly related to how direct you can be to other people.

How to Handle Mini-Crises

One thing that you can always count on is that if something can go wrong, it most likely will. As an employee who will truly stand out in the crowd, have a backup plan on hand for almost any circumstance that can arise.

Any time you are planning a presentation, a conference, or any type of activity that is important to your company (and aren't they all?), plan ahead for everything that can possibly go wrong. For example:

1. Do you have on hand new bulbs for any type of projector or equipment that might require a replacement at some point in time?

2. Do you have backup equipment such as laptops to be used for power point presentations?

3. Do you have your presentations backed up in case of a failure of one of the systems?

4. Do you have the charts and graphs backed up in case they get lost, stolen, or damaged?

5. Do you have all of the material on your computer backed up?

6. Do you know the name and number of a specialist who can make immediate on-site calls in case of a crash and lost material?

7. Do you know the name and number of repair people in case of a crash of other types of crucial equipment, such as air conditioning, heating systems, or electricity?

8. Do you know the name, number, and location of copy shops so that they can be contacted for short-term printing?

9. Do you know the name of a temporary employment agency when someone is unable to fulfill their duties on short-term notice and must immediately be replaced?

10. Do you know the name and number of backup people for conferences, catering, hotels, restaurants, transportation, travel agencies, etc., if you should need to make changes on short notice?

There are many other types of information that can and probably will become useful. When you are working on a presentation for a client or company, prepare a list of all backup information for anything that can go wrong. Don't count on any day becoming a stress-free day. It is not likely to happen.

Proofread! Proofread! Proofread!

Good Writing Skills are Essential

In teaching communication skills at the college level, I have never ceased to be amazed at how many graduating seniors have such poor English skill levels. To get a degree in business, you are always required to take basic English composition and business English. It should be required for all degrees. If you cannot communicate effectively with your clients, customers, or co-workers, you are at a great disadvantage in any type of progression through the company. Whether you are writing inter-office memos or correspondence to clients, designing materials, or keeping records, the manner in which you put the information together is a direct reflection on your ability to effectively communicate.

How to Write for Excellent Communication

1. **Put your information in sequential order.** This makes it easier for the reader to follow and absorb.

2. **Briefly summarize** all the information in the first paragraph.

3. **Avoid wordiness.** Say what you want to say in simple terms.

4. **Use simple language.** Most information in newspapers, books, etc., is written at a 7th grade reading level. This prevents the majority of readers from having to stop and figure out exactly what the writer is trying to say.

5. **Don't use jargon.** If you are writing to a person who is in the same field as you, the jargon may be appropriate. If, however, you are writing to a customer or client or someone in another division of your organization, it is unlikely that jargon will do anything but confuse or frustrate them.

6. **Avoid clichés** in most instances. The simpler the better for most writing.

7. **Don't be redundant.** You do not have to tell someone that the meeting is at 12 noon. It is not likely that it is going to be at midnight.

8. **Use good grammar.** Strunk and White's *Elements of Style* is available on the web. I have a 20,000-word spelling dictionary in my desk that I have used since college. Keep information such as that or a full dictionary and thesaurus handy at all times. (This is also available on the web.)

9. **Proofread everything**—several times. Spell checks and grammar checks don't always pick up words if they happen to be used in the wrong context. Reread everything yourself, or have someone else read it for you. If possible, let it rest a bit and then reread it. Sometimes you will see errors at a later time that you would miss if you had just completed the material.

10. **Request action.** If any action needs to be taken by the recipient, it should be stated in the last paragraph of the transmission.

11. **Continuously learn.** We can always improve on the skills that we use. You are either moving forward or backward in your abilities. You never stand still.

You Can Handle the Computer

My grandson asked me a few days ago about the computer that I had when I was young. I told him that we didn't have a computer. He paused a moment and said, "I know that it was really different, but what exactly did it look like?" I again told him that I didn't have a computer.

After the fourth round of this conversation, his eyes got very large, and he said to me in a very astonished tone, "You had no computer? What are you, older than dirt?"

Well, I may be, but we had no computer, and I can remember being as astonished as he was the first time my employer bought me an electric typewriter. I thought it was going to dominate my life.

You can imagine my challenge when, during my master's program, we were expected to work out programs on that gigantic, sterile room full of equipment that only took cards written in some foreign language that I did not speak. You would type forever on these 4-by-8-inch cards, and then when you got to the front of the long line to run them (about midnight), you would get back enough "trash" to paper your house if one, only one, of the cards was incorrect.

I promised myself that I would never touch another computer as long as I lived. Now, I live on the computer. So if you haven't tried it, you should. It is no longer quite so scary.

My dear husband took me into the computer age very gradually. The first book I wrote was done in long hand, and he convinced me to put the final touch on it by using what was then called a word processor. It was very similar to a Microsoft Word program with nothing else attached.

Of course, I loved it as it saved me so much time.   For writing the next book, he convinced me to get a computer. Well, I just recently convinced him to enlarge the size of the hard drive because it just wasn't big enough to handle all the work that I now use my computer for.

Computers are standard in most classrooms, in most homes, and in almost any type of business now. Whether you are trying to get a job at a bank or a library or an auto parts store, you will need basic computer literacy.

Computer literacy means you need to be able to walk up to one without looking horrified and do some simple tasks.

Computer literacy does not mean that you have to be able to write a program or network computers. It simply means that you need to be able to walk up to one without looking horrified and do simple tasks such as opening and closing a file, using a word processing program, and sending and receiving emails. If you need more advanced knowledge, the job requirements will specify those requirements, and if need be, you can take a course to upgrade your skills.

Basic computer skill programs are offered through most school districts, community colleges, and sometimes through your library. The fees are usually minimal. Career training programs are also offered through the local Labor Department Office, and these classes are frequently free.

If you don't have a computer, check your local library. They will most likely have one that you can use for Internet access. Through that access you can check on websites for free online courses. GCF Global Learning offers free online courses, and so does HP Learning Center. It does not take long to pick up some very basic computer skills and prevent yourself from being known as someone who is "older than dirt."

"Technology" is Not a Scary Word

We live in the era of rapidly increasing technology in a global economy. Things are changing so rapidly that your cell phone may become obsolete within six months, or you may seem way out of date because you are still using a cell phone instead of an iPhone or a Blackberry. It is very challenging to stay up to date.

Larger corporations frequently offer courses to help update your skills. Never assume that you simply don't need to learn a new technology. As it happens, that will usually be the one you will need the most the next time an advancement opportunity is presented. Keep learning.

My grandfather lived 101 years, and he traveled in everything from a covered wagon to a jet airplane. As drastic as that seems, the technological advancement during those 101 years cannot touch the rapid changes that are taking place today. If you make a choice to quit learning, your skills will become antiquated more rapidly than you can believe. Your opportunities for advancement and promotion will go to a standstill. Continuous learning is essential for continued growth.

Learn How and When to Delegate

You do not have to do everything. Surprised? Sometimes you act like it. Sometimes you act like it is impossible to say "No" to people. Both professionally and personally, we have to learn how and when to say, "No."

Don't try to do things that you are not interested in. You simply can't do everything, and you have to pick and choose the things that are most important to you. Make choices that fit inside of your priorities, your goals, your dreams, and your idea for living. Someone else's priorities, someone else's goals may not be the same as yours.

Learn how and when to say "No."

If a request breaks your concentration or your focus on what you are trying to do, then it can be very damaging to the project you happen to be working on. Learn how to turn down those obligations if it happens to be a choice for you. A lot of professional obligations we have to accept, but all of those personal opportunities do not have to be accepted. Remember, it is okay to say "No" and not feel guilty.

The Art of Delegating

When professional requests or opportunities come in that you choose not to accept, it may become a good time to learn the art of delegating. Rule Number 1 in delegating is that you never do something for yourself that you can get someone else to do for you. Professionally we talk about the elephants and the ants. The elephants are things that you have to do, that only you can do, that you are totally responsible for, that you have to make a decision about, or that you have to take action on and be directly involved in. The ants are the things that you could do but that someone else also could do. These are the things that you delegate. That same rule applies in your personal life.

Decide to become the master of your time and not the slave of it. Delegation will increase your productivity. However, you must always remember that even though in your delegation you have instructed someone what you want done and how and when you want it done, it may not be done precisely as you would have accomplished it yourself. Before blowing up, look over the situation carefully, and remind yourself that just because something is different does not necessarily make it wrong.

Delegation increase productivity

The most significant delegating step is to tell the person to whom you are delegating why this particular project needs to be done. People are much more interested in making things happen if they know how they fit into the big picture.

People often do not delegate because of their own insecurity. They are afraid that if they teach their assistant how to accomplish even the most menial of tasks, they will lose their jobs. If that happens, your job was probably in jeopardy anyway. What should, and most likely will happen, is that the powers that be will see how good you are at working with others to accomplish larger and more important tasks in a timely manner and will consider you for a more important position.

Unless you learn to delegate, you will not have time to accomplish your dreams, goals, and objectives. Failure to delegate is like going out and buying a watch dog and then coming home and doing all the barking yourself. When you delegate you are giving others an opportunity to learn and grow. When they learn and grow, so will you.

Your time is your life. If you waste your time, you waste your life. If you make the most of your time, you will make the most of your life. The choice is yours.

H.E.L.P.

Go to www.howtogetandkeepajob.com for free work pages:
What I need to work on evaluation sheet

Notes

CHAPTER 10
Skill No. 7 - Budgeting

Take time to smile; we all need a good
break to lighten up the midweek crisis.

Author unknown

How Do I Live on My Salary?

First and most important, if you cannot live on your salary and manage your budget at home, why would any corporation want you to manage theirs?

This is important. If you choose to become a professional and are looking for advancement in your company, you must manage yourself first.   If you agree, keep reading. If you already have and live successfully on a budget, you may not need this skill but might find some additional ideas that would add to your efficiency. If you are in debt up to your eyeballs and are wondering how to make it to payday without a promotion or a raise, you had better keep reading.

Everyone should be living on a budget. Corporations cannot function without a budget, and a household is just a mini-corporation. If you have absolutely no idea how to design one, take a quick trip to the bookstore or your local library and check on a household budget book. Look online. There are great resources there. Mint.com provides a solid budgeting helper, and I'm sure there are many others. It will help you see where you are currently spending your money and where you are wasting it. It will give you some percentages to work with: how much of your salary should be used for housing, utilities, travel, food, insurance, savings, etc.

Homes

There is an old saying that people have to keep up with the Joneses. Forget the Joneses. Live where you can afford to live. If you cannot afford a home at this point, move into an apartment and put money aside each month until you can get into even a small home. Then, as you repair it and increase the value by making it look inviting, put a "For Sale" sign out front and wait for someone to come along and desire it. You are in no hurry. I had friends who did this when they first married. They started in a very small home, made it look nice with a little yard work, paint, and basic repairs, and when it sold, they took the profit, added it to a new home, and started over again. They now live in a very large and lovely home, and it is well within their budget.

Cars

The same is true for cars. Don't drive a Lexus or a BMW because your friend does. Drive a good, safe car that serves its purpose, that is, to get you safely to and from work and necessary appointments. We do not need to compete with others. The life you are living is your own and is for you and your family. It is not to become a show for others.

Live where and how you can afford to live.

When our grandson began to drive and needed a car to go back and forth to school and work, he paid $2000 for one, and he and his dad did some basic work on it. They have added some repairs over the last couple of years, and although he does not have a new car, he has a good car, and it certainly serves its purpose. It is worth a great deal more than $2000 at this point.

If you are not handy with that type of work, find a friend who is, and trade off some talents. Maybe you can trim his yard or redo her flower beds in exchange for some basic car repairs.

When I was in college, we used to pool our talents and supplies all the time. We certainly would not have had as many good meals if we had not pooled our food. We had no problem doing this. We knew that we were working for our future and that one day it would no longer be necessary to share, but right then, it was—and it was okay. When times are tough, we need to work together and lean on each other. We all have our talents; pool them.

Food

Back to basics. That is the most powerful thought I can share about your food budget. Too many of us have grown accustomed to buying prepared foods, fast foods, and eating out. When we first started our home, we didn't have the money to do any of those things. When the economy is tight or when layoffs take place, the same thing happens. It is time to go back to basics.

When I was in college, I could have easily written a book titled *1001 Ways to Prepare Hamburger.* Hamburger was cheap then. I also learned how to prepare tongue because it was really cheap. (By the way, if you can get past the smell when you cook it, it makes very good cold sandwiches.) I learned how to grow vegetables from seeds—not those expensive little plants. And, I learned how to can. My grandson still talks about the wonderful homemade strawberry jelly I used to make.

Preparing fruits and vegetables in season and freezing or canning them is a tremendous time- and cost-saver. It is also an excellent way to avoid running to the fast- food joints on the way home from work. When you have food ready in the freezer, it is an easier decision to go home for dinner.

When both my husband and I had full time jobs, I would spend two Saturdays a month cooking. I would double my recipes and fix two casseroles or two roasts or two cobblers. One was ready for us to have that week and the next was in the freezer for later that month. I also learned how to be very creative with leftovers. They can easily be turned into vegetable soup or stews. Add a little homemade cornbread and you have a great, cost-saving meal.

Where most people get in trouble with their food budget is the quick little stop at some place like Starbucks for a latte on the way to work. They don't seem to realize that in a month's time that latte can easily add up to $50 or $60. I have a friend who runs by McDonald's for a muffin and Coke every morning on the way to work. She is always complaining about money, and I so want to remind her of that $3 - $4 she is spending at McDonald's on the way to work each morning. That adds up.

Think before you spend money.

Do you smoke? Not only for your health, but also for your budget, **stop!** The last time I checked, those things were $4-$5 a pack! Think how much you could save in just one month without them. What else do you do? Do you buy a soft drink at a fast food restaurant when you could buy a bottle for a similar price? Do you drink Cokes instead of tea? Do you buy coffee, tea, or other beverages at a restaurant instead of drinking water? Have you ever stopped to figure out how much that is costing you? That is one of the most profitable items on any restaurant's menu, and you are paying for it!

Think! Basically, that is the whole idea. Think before you spend money. Ask yourself, "Do I really need this, or do I just want it?" There is a very big difference. And when you are on a budget, you can't afford the difference.

Shop markets, shop seasonally, prepare your own food from scratch, use coupons, check for sales, and have a garden. Sometimes you can save a lot of money if you will buy a half or a quarter of a calf and put it in the freezer. Check the price first. A freezer for the house or garage, even a used one, can be very cost-saving when it comes to food.

Above all, eat healthy. Concentrate on fruits and vegetables and not chips and soft drinks full of sugar. If you are in the process of looking for a job or are simply trying to live within your means, an overweight body, which will increase your risk for illness, is not the way to go. Large medical bills can destroy your savings, and thus your budget, about as quickly as anything.

Clothes

My husband and I have reached a point in our lives where we can easily afford most things that we want, although we are very conservative and live pretty frugally. (Maybe this comes from lots of years of practice.) We have enjoyed a number of cruises over the years. On cruise ships they usually have a couple of nights where you are invited to wear formal clothes. Since we do not party, I don't wear formal clothes at home. So when it comes time to go on a cruise, I usually hit the gently used shops. If you find a good one, they have beautiful clothes at much more reasonable prices. I have also found lovely formals at the closeout sales after graduation or New Year's.

I have friends who would never wear sale clothes. Personally, I have very few things in my wardrobe that I didn't buy on sale. I buy basic items and blend them together. If you use good taste, they can come from almost anywhere.

I had a gentleman come up to me recently and say, "That is a great looking outfit you have on. Of course, you always wear great-looking clothes. You can certainly tell you are married to a doctor." I simply smiled, said, "Thank you," and refrained from telling him that everything I had on that particular evening had come from Walmart.

If you need to dress professionally, buy a good basic suit – wherever you can find it. If the suit is a basic color and style, you can change the looks of it multiple times by simply changing the blouse or shirt or by adding jewelry or scarves for women or a different tie or an open-neck look for men. Men can also use the same slacks and slip on a sweater and have a whole new look. It does not take a large wardrobe to look good. Just be versatile.

When I was on the lecture tour, I was often gone for a week or ten days at a time. I never carried more than a carry-on bag. I had two suits and two blouses. The key was that they blended. That meant that I could wear the jacket with either skirt or either blouse. I was also very sure that the material would not wrinkle so that I did not have to spend a lot of time and money on pressing. I carried two pair of shoes—high heels and flats. This gave me an opportunity to deal with how much rest I had the night before and how tired my feet were from standing for 6 hours a day. The shoes were navy or black—whichever matched the suits for that week.

Buy basic clothes and blend them together.

If you can only afford one coat, get an all-weather one. This gives you something to wear in the winter with the lining and something that can also be used in the spring rains without the lining. Watch for end-of-season sales. If you buy basic clothes, the ones on sale at the end of this year will certainly be okay for the same season next year.

As for children, never hesitate to shop garage sales or thrift stores. Children, particularly small children, almost always grow out of their clothes before they wear them out. This is the only sensible place to get clothes for early childhood.

When they get to be teens and think they have to have fourteen pairs of name brand jeans, put them on a budget. My daughters always had a budget, and they had to buy everything with it, even their winter coat and their underwear. They thought it was fun to get that much money each month until they realized that it would not pay for a coat and that they would be required to save in order to get some of the items that they wanted. As a result, I have children who can pinch a penny about as far at it can be pinched.

Child Care

Child care is a very, very expensive item in the budget. Again, be creative. If you can work it out with a friend to share child care, it would save you a lot of money. Some are able to get a co-op going with a group of friends. Some husbands and wives are able to work different shifts, and some have decided that the one who makes the most money will work and the other will stay at home with the children.

The point is: discuss it. You definitely want what's best for your child. If one of you can stay at home, it is almost always the best solution, even if you have to sacrifice other things for that privilege. If not, be very careful what you decide to do. These are the formative ages of your children, and it is important what type of atmosphere they are spending their time in.

Health

Good health is an asset to not only your work environment but also to your personal family relationships. It doesn't happen by accident for most of us. It is an intentional act of caring. Exercise, eating right, and sleeping a sufficient number of hours is basically all that is required, and yet many people can't seem to put those three elements into their daily lives.

You only have one life and one body.
Do not take them for granted.

We have discussed food and food budgets in an earlier section, but that is not enough to keep you at the level of health where you are most productive. It is absolutely necessary to exercise. I know, you may be saying that there is just not room in the budget for a gym membership. Okay. But are there stairs in your home or in the building where you work? Do you use them? Is there a paved or dirt road in front of your home where you could walk either early in the morning or in the evening? Walking is the number one best exercise for all of us, and it is free. The only excuse that most of us have for not exercising is lack of self-discipline. Excuses are a dime a dozen, and if you want one to not exercise, it will always be readily available.

Sleeping is another essential element for good health. Just as we talked about in Chapter 5, there are times when our goals get out of balance, and we have to work through those times before we can rebalance them. That is normal. It is also normal during such times that we may become sleep deprived. Our bodies can handle that for brief periods of time, but over an extended period of time, it can cause great damage to our health. If you see that this is happening, it is essential that you make an adjustment and get things back in balance.

You only have one life and one body. Do not take them for granted.

Recreation

Be creative. Rent $1 movies and make popcorn for an evening of entertainment. Build your kids a swing out of an old tire. Mine was built out of the iron beams from an old car when I was growing up, and I loved it. Build them an obstacle course in the back yard, or a sand box, or stilts. Encourage them to draw and use the local library. Reading gives them eyes to the world.

What did you do when you were young? Not all of you had video games, Xboxes, or computers, and even if you did, was it always the best thing that you could have done with your time? How about playing in the sprinkler, or going to the park, or working in the flower beds? How about just spending time with your children? What it all boils down to, what children really want the most from their parents, is *time*. And while we are at it, isn't that what we want from each other as well? I love it when Robert and I *make* time for each other. We may just sit on the couch and talk, or share a book, or go riding. It doesn't matter what we do. What matters is that we are together, and we are making time for each other. Maybe that is one of the reasons that we have been married so long.

Watch the paper for free activities. Our museums and zoo will often have free days during holidays or on special occasions. Take advantage of those activities and share them with each other, your family, and your friends. Fun doesn't always have to cost money.

Education

If you want an education, it is available. Never say that you can't go to college. There are colleges where you pay no tuition and simply work your way through it, there are colleges that have work study programs, there are night schools, and there are many, many online programs. There are a large number of places today where you can obtain a degree without ever setting foot on a campus. That was not true a few years ago, but it is today. Check it out. It is also much more economical to go to school online than it is on campus.

You can go to school.
Don't ever give up that dream.

Also check with your company. Many companies, after a certain length of service time, will pay, or help pay, for you to go back to school. This is sometimes offered as part of the benefits package. It may be discussed with you during your interview. If not, it is certainly permissible for you to ask if such a benefit is available. The military will pay for you to go to school, and there are programs where the government or certain districts will pay your tuition if you will teach or practice in their area for a certain number of years after graduating.

You can go to school. Don't ever give up that dream. Yes, it will be hard, especially if you are working full time, but it can be done. I went to night school for three years while obtaining my bachelor's degree and worked full time and had a family. I was sometimes a little short of rest, but I could handle it because I knew that it was not going to last forever. I was also working full time and raising a family when I got my master's degree and my PhD. It can be done.

Insurance

Insurance, and retirement funds, and educational funds, and vacation funds.... there always seems to be something else to put money into. What is important to you? Who is going to take care of the bills and the family if you should get sick and have no insurance? Does that make it worth the sacrifice? You have to decide. Look carefully at all your options and make the best choice you can for you and your family. Check carefully on the people that you seek out for advice, and once you trust them, listen to their suggestions.

Vacations

Right out of college, I lived in a twin-city area. One was a white-collar city and one was a blue-collar city. The conversations were very different. When it came to vacation time, the blue-collar people would talk about going to the lake or camping out and maybe going to a national park somewhere close to where they lived. The white-collar people talked just as casually about flying to Europe, going on a Caribbean cruise, or skiing in Aspen.

The point is, they were both going on vacations. They were just different. It did not mean that one had a better time than the other. It was just different.

Once again, we stay within our means. If that says to you that this year for vacation we are going to camp out in the back yard that is okay. Just make it fun, and it will be a memorable experience for a lifetime. Memories are not always made of money. Some of our best memories when the kids were growing up were not of the most expensive restaurants we ate in, but of some of the worst ones we shared. Some of our best vacations were when we went to a local lake and took the kids skiing on a friend's boat or went fishing from the shore.

Memories are not always made out of money.

One Christmas recently we were talking about memories, and I asked the girls what they remembered about one long, well-planned, and rather expensive vacation that we had taken when they were pre-teens. They looked at each other and started laughing. Finally they looked at us and said, "The only thing we remember about that trip is how tired we got." We should have stayed home and fished at the lake again.

Investments

Once you have a job and are developing a budget within which you and your family can successfully live, it is essential to begin some investment into the future. The first step is to have enough ready cash for emergencies. This money should be held in a liquid, interest-earning savings account or money market account. (Liquid assets are investments that can be turned into cash very quickly and easily.) It is recommended by most investment counselors that you have at least six months worth of expenses times 120%.

According to Tracy Hancuff, Vice President for Merrill Lynch, once this primary requirement is met, the next important step for investment planning is to participate in a 401K or other retirement plan. If your company has a 401K and does matching contributions, you should make this a priority. The employer-matching contributions are considered free money as long as you become vested in the plan.

If you do not have access to a 401K or other work-sponsored retirement plan, then an IRA would be the next best choice. Roth IRAs and Regular IRAs are great tools for long-term retirement planning. These accounts can be opened at banks, mutual fund companies, and brokerage firms.

If you find this confusing, then find a wealth management advisor whom you can trust. Talk with your friends and find out who they use. Interview prospects and ask lots of questions. Discuss the type of investments that you are willing to risk. Above all, remember that this is your future, it is your money, and you have the right to make choices about it.

Frugality

I guess I am a rarity, but I don't like to shop. My husband says that he is very grateful. I have friends who think that they have to have a new wardrobe every year. That would bore me to tears. I am very happy with what I have, and if I happen to be in a store and happen to see something on a very good sale, I will usually add it to my collection to give it a little update, but it is rarely an intentional event.

Shop off season for better buys.

I shop off season for most everything. I buy Christmas all year. I have a very secure budget for Christmas, and I like to give my family as much value for their allowance as possible. So, if I can buy a $120 sweater for $12 in July, I grab it. My goal is to be finished with all of my shopping by September 1st so that I don't have to put stress on myself and my family during the holiday season. I get to enjoy the decorations, the music, and the lights. I try to never be the one racing through the stores. This goal saves me not only time but money.

I also buy wedding and graduation gifts the same way. When I find a generic type of gift at a reasonable price, I try to pick it up. I learned this when the children were little and seemed to always forget to tell me that the birthday party for Johnny was that afternoon at 4. I started keeping a stash so that I could grab a gift and we could be off for the party on time.

Last night my hubby said, "By the way, did I tell you that we are invited to a dinner tonight for one of the staff who is getting married?" If he did, I didn't remember it, and I had one hour to get ready and prepare a gift. Fortunately my stash had a lovely set of taupe placemats and napkins in it, and the bride loved them. "They will go perfectly with my new dishes," she said. Why not—they were taupe!

Some of the gifts that I gave when I could afford nothing else were homemade ones. People loved them so much that I still do that quite often. I made bookends out of chunks of glass that I found at a quarry. I put together checker sets by sanding and oiling pieces of wood from a building site and sewing together scrap fake fur for the large "floor" board. I have also used scrap fabric to make seasonal pillows, vests, and pillowcases. (You can find a lot of fabric at garage sales as well as other very nice items.) Be creative. If you don't know how to knit the fashionable scarves, learn how. There are classes at most any store that carries yarn, and there are always friends who will be happy to help you. We all need to be needed.

Take care of what you have. I wash everything in cold water. I found out many years ago that it was just as safe as hot water, it saved on heating bills, and it was not nearly as harsh on my clothes. They don't fade or shrink nearly as fast as if they were put in hot water. I am very careful that they are hung up damp and hung up rapidly. Clothes will shrink less if you will let them get partially dry and hang them up to complete drying rather than leaving them in the dryer until they are bone dry.

I frequently spot-clean clothes instead of sending them to the cleaners. Sometimes we just get a dot of something on perfectly clean clothes, and they can be quickly spotted and be wearable again without the additional expense of cleaning.

Bartering

My husband and I have always bartered when we could. I have been fortunate to have received a lot of lovely jewelry since we have been married because Robert happened to have had a patient who was a jeweler and wanted to barter. Yeah! We also bartered with other patients, and I did some on my own. I would type a thesis in exchange for someone cleaning my house or put data into a computer program in exchange for help with the statistical part of my thesis.

Bartering is a great way to get quality products and help without having to come up with actual cash—your services for theirs. This has been going on since the beginning of marketing, and it is still just as valid.

Quick Tips

If you find yourself with more bills than you can pay, talk to your creditors. Generally they will work with you, particularly if you contact them when you first recognize the challenge and don't wait until your situation is totally beyond repair.

IF you use credit cards, pay them off every month.

IF you use credit cards, pay them off every month. If you cannot discipline yourself to do that or cannot afford to do that, **tear them up!** This is essential if you ever plan to live within your means.

Keep track of *every* penny that each of you spends for a period of one week. If you put a quarter in the candy machine, write it down. If you buy an extra cup of coffee at lunch, don't forget to add it to the lunch tab. After a week or so, you will realize where your money is going and can begin to make adjustments.

If you don't know how to balance your bank account, go by the bank and ask them to teach you. They will be more than happy to do so. I worked for a bank right out of college, and more people than you can imagine asked for that type of guidance. Not being able to keep your bank account in balance can destroy your budget and your credit. If you just look at the bank statement or call the bank and ask for a balance and then write a check based on that amount of money, you may be seriously overdrawing your account and bouncing the checks that have not yet cleared. This can cost you a great deal of extra money in overdrafts and a serious loss of credit from those who receive returned checks from you.

It is not terribly hard to get credit and have a good credit rating, but it is very difficult to correct a bad one.

H.E.L.P.

Go to www.howtogetandkeepajob.com for free work pages:
Personal budget worksheet

CHAPTER 11
Skill No. 8 - Stress Management

Life is not about waiting for the storm to pass.
It is about learning to dance in the rain.

Vivian Green

Make Stress Work for You and Not Against You

If someone picked up this book, saw the name of this chapter, and then immediately handed it to you, it might be a good sign that you have stress in your life. I have written two books on simplified stress-management techniques and occasionally my husband will say, "Have you read your books lately?" Wonder what he is trying to tell me? Surely "I" couldn't have stress. I wrote my dissertation on that!

Well, I do. So does everyone else, and it is not always bad. Chuck Yeager said that he never let a day go by that he didn't have fun or learn something. That is a great way to live, and I hope I can do that until the day I die.

75% of all illnesses are either directly or indirectly related to stress.

Dealing with stress is a learned skill. It is a part of our lives every day. It is our internal response to pressure. Whether it is good or bad is based a great deal on the way we look at it. Stress in itself is not dangerous; it is the way that we respond to it that can make it dangerous. We all have pressures in our lives. It is when we allow those pressures to become "gottas" that they become dangerous. You know that one— you "gotta" do this and you "gotta" do that.

There are four things about stress that are not going to change:

1. **Stress is here to stay.**

2. **Situations do not cause stress.**

3. **We can respond or react—our choice.**

4. **We have unique stress symptoms.**

When we do face a stressful situation, we have three choices: 1) fight it (confront it), 2) take flight (run), or 3) adapt (consider options). The key to stress management is realizing that we have these choices.

2 Types of Stress

We have two kinds of stress: **Distress** and **Eustress.** Stress is defined as the non-specific response of the body to any demand made upon it. Distress is when stress controls you, and Eustress is when you control your own stress.

It is a known fact that at least 75% of all illnesses are either directly or indirectly related to stress, and that includes everything from cavities to cancer. At least 50 % of the population suffers from one stress symptom regularly. We can make stress work for us or against us. It is up to us.

For example: Let's say you get a call at 10 o'clock that your new client is coming in to view the contract at 12. One of two things are going to happen: 1) Distress says that you don't have the contract finished, you are going to rush through it, maybe make some mistakes, and be completely stressed by the time the client arrives. 2) Eustress says that you have been practicing your time management techniques and can spend the two hours prior to your client's arrival straightening your office, having a casual cup of coffee, and reviewing the details of the contract. Which is to your advantage?

Distress

When we *choose* to allow Distress in our lives, we can react physically, psychologically, or physiologically. Look at this list of stress symptoms and see how many you recognize. Please don't tell me you have all of them. If so, just call 911. You are going to need them sooner rather than later.

Headaches

Muscle aches

Chronic illnesses (colds, flu, allergies, etc.)

Anxiety

Depression

Emotional ups and downs

Irritability

Increase in the level of smoking

Drug or alcohol abuse

Insomnia or too much sleep

Compulsive eating or dieting

Ulcers or diarrhea

Indigestion or vomiting

High blood pressure

Heart attack

Stroke

Sexual dysfunction

Unsolved challenges at home or at work

Eustress

If we can turn our challenges into Eustress, it can not only make our lives easier, but it can also make it much more productive.

Eustress is what will help you get the new curtains in the guest bedroom that you have been procrastinating about. Your mother is coming next week, and you don't want her to see your bare windows.

Eustress is our good stress.

Eustress will help you – finally – get the garage cleaned out. The savings account says that you now have enough money for a new car, and you certainly are not going to leave it out in the bad weather.

That extra surge of energy, that ability to destroy your procrastination, that desire to do better, are all created by eustress. Eustress is our good stress.

When to Use Positive Self-Talk

We cannot always change our jobs or the situation or the responsibilities that we have in our lives, but we can change our responses. Sometimes the change of response can change our stress from distress to eustress. Let's look at these 7 types of stressors and see how we can use positive self-talk to make that change.

1. **Fear:**
   a. First things first.
   b. Easy does it.
2. **Lack of Appreciation:**
   a. Don't take it personally.
   b. Let it go.

3. **Boredom:**

   a. Go for it.

   b. Plan B.

4. **Lack of Support:**

   a. First things first.

   b. Keep it simple.

5. **Unclear Responsibilities:**

   a. It doesn't matter.

   b. Don't take it personally.

6. **Overload:**

   a. One day at a time.

   b. Plan B.

7. **Lack of Control:**

   a. Let it go.

   b. Keep it simple.

In every challenging situation, we have a choice of whether we will respond or react. If the challenge was caused by a personal interaction, we need to keep in mind that we never know what the other person may be dealing with at this particular moment. They may be "kicking our cat" because we are convenient, not because they picked us out to receive their anger.

Stress can cause conceptual blindness or tunnel vision. When we are under distress, it is not a good time to make a decision. Making a decision when we are under extreme pressure or with the wrong attitude can affect the rest of our lives. Back off until you feel more under control and can choose to respond instead of react.

Workaholism Is Devastating

Workaholism is a symptom of negative stress management. It is very closely related to time management. It usually means one of two things: you are allowing too much time for any particular project, and we all know that any job will fit the amount of time allotted to it; or you are procrastinating and allowing so many things to get in your way that it is impossible to meet a deadline on time.

Either of those issues can and must be eliminated. This type of work style is not only devastating to you and your organization, but it is also devastating to your personal life and family life as well.

If this is an issue for you, (and someone has probably complained about it if it is), then Chapter 8 is crucial information for you. Take it very seriously.

Workaholism is a symptom of negative stress management.

If no one has complained, and you are putting in way too many hours—long days, evenings, weekends, and no vacations—then either you have been away from home so much that they no longer need or miss you because they have become accustomed to life without you, or the boss is loving it that you have taken on so much of his work responsibility that he/she is now able to spend more time with his/her family. Which is it?

Do a time-management study on you. Write down what you do in 15-minute increments for a period of one week. Be honest. You may be shocked at how much time you are spending actually working. On the other hand, you may be shocked to realize how you have allowed yourself to become over obligated in your work load because of your inability to say, "No."

I have a sign on my desk that says, "What part of 'No' do you not understand?" It is an important sign. I read it often. It is extremely easy for me to over-obligate myself because I enjoy so many different things. Fortunately I have a husband who is also a regulator of my time and energy. I have recorded two albums on stress and time management and written two books on those topics, and when I begin to overload, he will casually mention that I should make time to read one of my books, or he will drop one on the middle of my desk. It is just a gentle reminder to take a closer look at my schedule and see what I am doing to myself.

When I was writing my dissertation, Robert walked in one day and said, "Honey, I have this great idea! Why don't we turn the kitchen into a library? The oven would make a wonderful book case. It is safe and compact, and it does seem a shame to have such a large room in the house that never gets used."

Hummmm! I decided that I would prove him wrong, that I could do it all. So I did a time management study on myself (just like the one I recommended above) and discovered that *if* I were going to cook, I would have 15 minutes that I could spare for the kitchen. In those days I really was an overachiever, so I made the decision that 15 minutes would work, and I wrote a *15 Minute Recipes* cookbook.

Interestingly enough, it was so popular that it sold thousands, and people wanted a diet cookbook, so I wrote *15 Minute Diet Recipes*. The next year they asked for another new book, and I wrote *31 Quick & Easy Snazzy Meals*. After the popularity of those three, I closed my cookbook writing career with *My Favorite Recipes*.

Hopefully your time-management study will prove to be more successful than mine because even though I discovered exactly what I needed to do to solve my challenge, it ended up taking me into a new career, and I never did get back to the kitchen. (I surely do have some good recipes, though!)

If you have discovered that time-management, procrastination, or over-extension are not your challenges, then it may be perfectionism. Whatever it is, for the sanity of you and your family, work it out.

Perfectionism Is Unnecessary

No one is perfect. It is impossible to be perfect. But you can be excellent, and when you accept that concept, it makes life a great deal easier.

There was only one person in the universe who was ever perfect, and it was not you. However, some people spend a great deal of wasted time trying to become that person. If you do, you will find that you do not consider anything that you accomplish to be good enough.

Eventually this type of attitude will destroy your self-confidence and cause you to become dissatisfied with every aspect of your life. If you procrastinate, if you refuse to take risks and/or if you spend an over abundant amount of time on menial tasks, you are headed toward perfectionism.

I love to paint. I don't get to do nearly as much of it as I would like to any more, but it is something that I enjoy very much. When I first started painting, I would go to a studio and spend one day a week doing nothing but painting. I would choose my topic for the day, prepare my canvas, select the colors and needed brushes, and then begin. I would paint and paint and paint. The painting would become quite good and then, the longer the day got, the worse the painting became. By the end of the day, I would often have a major mess.

After having returned a number of times to get the necessary help to restore my paintings, the instructor came to me one day and said, "Donna, when you are painting, I want you to start quitting just before you finish. You are working the paintings to death. Enough is enough."

I can look back at so many of the things that I have done in my life and realize that I had "worked them to death." His encouragement has become my motto. This book will be good when it is finished, but it will not be perfect. My goal is for it to be sufficiently put together to help you get and keep a job. If I can accomplish that goal, then I won't need to do any more. Enough is enough.

Excellence versus Perfectionism

Many people think that the word "excellent" means "perfect." **Not true!**

During the many years that I was on the lecture circuit, I would receive sometimes 300 to 500 evaluations per day. They all counted just as much as the one you get once a quarter or once a year. Not only the people I contracted with, but also the people who paid to listen to me speak, expected me to be perfect. I couldn't do that. So I learned to become excellent.

You can never be perfect, but you can be excellent every day.

What the word "excellent" means is that you give all that you have to give that day – in that set of circumstances, under those conditions, at that point of time in your life – you give it your all. You may not be as good today as you were yesterday or as good today as you will be tomorrow, but when you give it all you have today, you have been excellent. Whew! Doesn't that feel better?

It doesn't let you off the hook. In fact, it probably requires more of you than you are used to giving because it does not say that you are excellent if you give all that you have to give *once in a while*. It says, "every day."

I got excellent ratings because that was my goal every day, and that was what I did. I would walk out of that conference so exhausted some days that I could barely get to the airport, but I knew that I had given it my all. That is what excellent means.

You can become excellent, and you can do it without becoming a perfectionist or a workaholic. Make a habit of giving everything that you have to everything that you do, but understand at what point enough is enough. Establish some priorities and set some time limits before you allow yourself to experience burnout.

How to Avoid Burnout

Perfectionism, overextension, and workaholism can all lead to burnout. Watch for symptoms before you allow burnout to destroy your job or career. If you suddenly become dissatisfied with your job – for no apparent reason – and lose interest in your work and your life, you may be experiencing burnout.

Watch for these symptoms:

1. **Do you dread going to work more than usual?**
2. **Have you become cynical?**
3. **Are you restless and bored even with things you used to enjoy?**
4. **Are you forgetful?**
5. **Are you tired all of the time?**
6. **Are you sick more than usual?**
7. **Do you feel like you are working harder and accomplishing less?**
8. **Do you ever feel panicky?**
9. **Do you feel unhappy for no apparent reason?**

If you answered "Yes" to most of these questions, you are probably experiencing burnout. You may have tried to become everything to everybody and, as a result, are accomplishing less and feeling massively unappreciated. Either that or you have stopped learning and allowed your life to become stagnant.

Perfectionism, overextension, and workaholism can all lead to burnout.

Burnout can be very dangerous. It can cause you to have serious physical problems. It causes fatigue and a decrease in your immune system which results in your inability to fight off disease. The emotional aspect can cause you to feel trapped and helpless and may cause you to make decisions that you might later regret. It can also do a major job on your positive attitude. Remember the one we worked so hard on in Chapter 4? All of the things that come about as a result of a negative attitude can pop right back into place once again. Don't let this happen.

In Chapter 5, we talked extensively about goals and their importance. One of the elements of goal-setting is to set them in all areas of your life, and we looked at what happens when the goals in one area get totally out of balance. The result can easily become burnout. Over-working, over-committing, and not taking care of yourself can throw your life completely out of balance and create a vibrant atmosphere for burnout. If you recognize any signs of potential burnout, take corrective steps right away before the physical, emotional, and mental aspects of your life pay the price.

25 Ways to Be Good to Yourself

In Mathew 22:39 Jesus tells us that the second greatest commandment is to "love your neighbor as yourself." In other words, if we do not know how to take care of ourselves, we cannot adequately take care of our family, friends, and neighbors.

The majority of illnesses in this country are the result of an unhealthy lifestyle. It does not always take big changes to make a significant difference. Many times, it is the little things that result in the biggest improvement in our health and outlook on life.

Try these simple suggestions for revitalizing your energy and personal productivity. You have nothing to lose and may regain your life.

1. **Establish uninterrupted quiet time – each day – to accomplish specific tasks.** You will find that your production level will increase and your stress level will decrease because you are actually getting something done.

2. **Take a walk instead of a coffee break.** Physical activity vents excess pressure. Walking is one of the most effective aerobic exercises and one that almost everyone can do. It is also a wonderful way to stimulate creative thinking. When there is time to get past that first mile, you will find your mind just flows with ideas.

3. **Make a checklist for tomorrow.** At the end of each day, before you leave your work area, make a list of the six most important things to do the following day. Arrange these tasks in the order of their importance. Each morning, begin with the first item on your list, and scratch it off when you are finished. Work your way right down the list. If you do not finish an item, put it on the list for the following day.

4. **Take a mini-vacation every four hours during the day.** Get up. Walk around. Look out the window. Daydream for a few minutes. Get a drink of water. The purpose is to move around both mentally and physically for just a few minutes.

5. **Get the sleep that you need.** Lack of sleep can make you more susceptible to stress and more irritable. The amount of sleep you require may be very different from that of others. Do not try to judge how much sleep or rest you should have based on someone else's needs. Get the amount that you need. You know your body better than anyone else. Pay attention to it.

6. **See failures as learning experiences instead of roadblocks.** Look at the situation as another experience that can help you grow.

7. **Un-clutter your life.** Get rid of the stuff you never use—those clothes you never wear, books that only sit on your shelf. Drop memberships in organizations in which participating has become an unpleasant chore. Cancel subscriptions to magazines you do not read.

8. **Spend time with special friends.** Do something enjoyable with the special people in your world at least twice a month. Remember to smile, laugh, have fun, and enjoy life with each other. Enjoy dinner with "thinking" friends. Important: Set aside specific time for the significant people in your world. If you do not, other things will fill your schedule.

9. **Be kind to others.** What goes around comes around. When you are kind to other people, they will be kind to you.

10. **Do not be afraid of change.** Do not let anyone tell you that you cannot do something because it has never been done. That is the time to begin.

Little things can revitalize your energy and outlook on life.

11. **Explore your talents.** Are you great at building friendships? Making peace? Do you make people feel good? Make a list of what you are good at, and post it where you can see it the first thing every morning. Start the day knowing how special you are.

12. **Create a wish bank.** Find a special box or jar and create a wish bank for yourself. Make a list of things you would like to do but just never seem to get around to. Put some 5-minute items in there. Add some 10-minute ideas or maybe some 15- or 30-minute items. Then, periodically draw out a wish card and make it come true.

13. **Give the gift of time.** The greatest gift you can give to anyone, including yourself, is the gift of time. We all receive 86,400 seconds a day. We either use them or lose them. Because time is so precious and cannot be expanded, when we share it with someone else, we give them a rare and beautiful gift.

14. **Be a kid again.** Sometimes, as adults, we are so afraid that someone is going to see us that we forget how to enjoy and just be. Find a pile of dried leaves and listen to them crunch as you walk through them. Walk barefoot on grass that is still covered with early morning dew. For one day, leave your inhibitions behind and be a child again.

15. **Touch the earth.** Plant some flowers in your flowerbed or window box. Improve the beauty in your world. Dig in the dirt. Let the soft, moist soil run through your fingers. There is something very peaceful about working with the earth.

The greatest gift you can give to anyone, including yourself, is the gift of time.

16. **Daydream.** Take a moment now and then to dream about something that you very much want to have happen. Visualize it in the greatest of detail—the colors, the sounds, the smells, the sights—exactly as you wish it to happen.

17. **Buy a gift for yourself – for no reason at all.** Have it gift-wrapped, and then take your time unwrapping it.

18. **Take a joy break.** Sometimes we just need to laugh. Keep a drawer or box with articles, jokes, and stories that will tickle your funny bone. Your mind will work better, and you will be much more productive when you laugh while you work.

19. **Think in terms of right now.** During the day, stop and ask yourself, "Is there a better way, right now, for me to take care of me?" The answer to this question may be to relax your shoulders, take a walk, switch projects, tackle something you have been putting off, have someone help you lift something, or maybe take a lunch break.

20. **Act enthusiastic.** Do not save enthusiasm for special occasions. Use it now. Share it with everyone you meet.

21. **Send yourself flowers.** Do not forget the card. Write a very special message on it and sign it, "An admirer."

22. **Un-plan an evening.** Set aside one evening a week that is totally unplanned—time when you can do anything you want to do.

23. **Limit your pity parties.** If you must have one at all, limit it to one a week and make sure it lasts no longer than 15 minutes. Put on some sad music and really get in tune with your emotions. Cry. Feel sorry for yourself. Review all the depressing situations you can come up with. But be sure to set a timer, because when 15 minutes have passed, you are finished for the week.

24. **Live in the moment.** Too often, we try to live yesterday, today, and tomorrow at the same time. We cannot do that. Tomorrow is only a promissory note. All we have is today—right now. We need to learn to live one day and even one moment at a time because this is all we have. Nothing else is certain.

25. **Believe in you.** You are unique. You can do things no one else can do. You can be things no one else can be. You touch the lives of other people in a way that only you can. You are here for a very important reason. Your purpose in this world can be fulfilled by no one else.

H.E.L.P.

Go to www.howtogetandkeepajob.com for free work pages:
Stress test

Section III

How to be on the Competitive Edge

Remember, life is too short

to skip the chocolate.

Author unknown

Notes

CHAPTER 12
Communication Skills

I know you understand what you think I said, but I am not
sure you realize that what you hear is not what I meant.

Robert McCloskey

The Age of Technology

Look around you…the United States is in the grip of a revolution. Although no shots ring out, the revolution is just as real and will have just as tremendous an influence on all the lives of Americans as an armed revolution would.

The revolution we are engaged in is the Social Revolution. It is the biggest revolution since the Industrial Revolution, and at center stage in this Social Revolution is the computer.

The top 10 in-demand jobs in 2010 did not exist in 2004.

When the first major computer was built in the mid 1940s, it contained 18,000 vacuum tubes, weighed 5 tons, occupied 6 rooms, and could process 10,000 instructions per second. It cost more than 5 million dollars to build. In 1980, more computing power was available on a piece of silicone 5 millimeters square and ½ inch thick. It cost less than $5 at the local electronic store.

If the aviation industry had made similar progress in the same 40 years, we would have been able to fly around the world for about two cents. The plane would have travelled at more than 1,000,000 miles per hour, and the trip would have taken about 80 seconds. Of course, genetics would also have had to be involved for us to fit into the plane, as it would have been about the size of a matchbox.

If it changed that much in the first 40 years, think about how much the information age has and is going to change in subsequent 40-year periods. Today, and probably far into the future, information is and will be the single largest factor in the U.S. labor force. Processing information is one of the major functions of managers and, with computers, can be done so much more efficiently and effectively that many layers of managers have been and are being reduced.

Between 1981 and 1988, half of the Fortune 1000 companies entirely eliminated at least one layer of management, and that was just the beginning. The information technology that we now have makes it possible to have speedier and much more efficient means of communication between crucial links in the organization and have research readily available for clients/customers that would have taken weeks to accumulate only a few years ago.

With the development of increasingly more efficient systems and databases gathering and analyzing information, routine corporate decision-making, done by mangers in the past, is now being done automatically. Computers are able to not only provide written analysis of data, but also to show trends and relate other information necessary for effective projection.

In 1980 only about ten percent of all households had personal computers. Today, that figure is closer to 90%. The computer age is reshaping the way we communicate. But we still have to consider the human factor. Generation Y is now outnumbering the Baby Boomers, and 96% of them have joined a social network. It is the Number 1 activity on the web.

Despite the fact that the entire contents of Webster's International Dictionary can be sent through an optic fiber in less than six seconds, the average speaker still speaks at the rate of 100-150 words per minute, and the average listener can only comprehend between 400-500 words per minute. The new technology cannot alter these human variables in the communication process. Technology is moving faster than anyone even dreamed 50 years ago. The rapidity with which newer and more sophisticated devices are developing is astounding, and yet this is only the beginning. Electronics that were state of the art six months ago are virtually obsolete today. We are learning and growing at a speed that is almost unbelievable. But as things change, they also remain the same.

The Information Revolution has reshaped the means by which we communicate but it has not and will not supplant the human link.

Even though social communication moves so rapidly that it took 38 years for radio to reach 50 million users and Facebook only nine months to reach 100 million users, the primary ways that people communicate are virtually the same today as they were 1000 years ago. We still respond not just to a voice but to the elements of a voice, soft or harsh, cold or warm, lilting or nasal. We still read each others' minds by facial expressions, gestures, and body language. We communicate not by just what is said, but also by *how* it is said. People have always desired speedier ways to communicate: carrier pigeons, the Pony Express, telegraph, telephones, satellites. And now a multitude of electronic devices are testaments to our desire to communicate instantly. Yet none of these means of communication have substantially altered the communication process itself, until now. Basic communication is still dependent on people, and it is still captured primarily in words and nonverbal cues. Although the Information Revolution has reshaped the means by which we communicate, it has done little to alter the necessary process. It has not and will not supplant the human link in communication.

Technology has not changed the fact that we still have to speak, write, and listen both verbally and nonverbally to decode the messages that we send to each other. However, it will be very interesting to see what the Millennial Generation and the potential Net Generation do to our communication. With the onset of Facebook, e-mail, and Twitter, we are losing our ability to share non-verbal communication. With that inability, our communication skills are cut to about 10 to 20%. We are seeing a change in written communication, which is the new generations' attempt to share tone, if not non-verbal skills. We are seeing more writing that is expressive: such things as "quotes," **bold,** CAPS, and exclamation marks "!" are appearing more frequently.

This inability to totally communicate, as we have done in the past, is probably the reason that technology such as YouTube, webinars, and webcast universities are becoming so popular. Once again, through those sources, we can not only hear the words, but we can also see and feel the emotion that is involved. The newest generation is so completely engrossed in technology that it will be very interesting to see how they change and/or confirm the importance of all areas of communication in the next few years. Our goal has to be that we will become better communicators in all areas of our lives and through all means that are available to us if we want to work with the international infrastructure of today. Time will only tell.

How do We Communicate?

Have you ever had anyone say to you, "It's not what you say; it is how you say it." Communication comes to us in three ways—through the words that we hear, through what we see, and through what we feel. Basically it is what we talked about in Chapter 7. When we are attempting to communicate, we are conveying our thoughts, feelings, and ideas into another mind that is receiving them based on their own experiences—their own thoughts, feelings, and ideas. Unless we are very careful, the reception of that information is going to be distorted by their experiences and emotions.

Communication can be a very complicated process. Listening is a learned skill. Speaking is also a learned skill, and that is why improving your communication skills will put you on the competitive edge of your career. So few people have the ability and/or desire to become accomplished at effectively communicating that it makes you a rarity in almost any field.

Communication is the cornerstone of every relationship. When it is clear and open, the relationship flourishes, and when it is blocked or muddled, it suffers. People who understand how communication functions in business, who have a wide repertoire of written and oral communication skills, and who know when and how to use those skills will advance more rapidly and contribute more fully to their organizations.

Communication is the cornerstone of every relationship. When it is clear and open, the relationship flourishes, and when it is blocked or muddled, it suffers.

A writer hopes that you will take the time to understand the written message. But a speaker must communicate clearly and in an understandable manner the first time. They do not get a second chance to convey their ideas. It is now or never. Maybe that is the reason that so many people say that they would rather die than make a presentation. Toastmasters International defines public speaking as "…not the result of eliminating those butterflies in your stomach, but simply getting them to fly in formation." And that is the skill to learn.

Overcoming the Fear of Communicating

As Williams Jennings Bryan, flanked by aides, approached the podium at the 1896 Democratic convention to accept his party's nomination for President of the United States, he muttered under his breath, "I wish God would strike me dead rather than have to give this speech." This quote came from a man who was considered to be one of the greatest American orators of history.

In Irving Wallace's *Book of Lists*, he reported that the American public's number one fear is the fear of public speaking. It affects everyone, famous or not, and the only difference is how they deal with it.

Former United States Vice President Alvin W. Barkley died while giving a speech. He may be the only one who ever actually died giving a speech. Public speaking is a safe experience. Although your knees are knocking, your heart is racing, your palms are sweating, your mouth feels like cotton, and your blood pressure is soaring, the odds are dramatically in your favor that you will survive. So let's get started.

H.E.L.P.

Check in the back of this book for additional helpful materials.

CHAPTER 13
How to Make Powerful Presentations

The highest reward for toil is not what you get from it,
but what you become by it.

John Ruskin

In the Wizard of Oz, Dorothy had an objective, a purpose. Her purpose was to get back home to Kansas. She knew what she wanted.

The most important purpose or goal of public speaking is to have a clear-cut objective. Confucius said, "The longest journey begins with one step." If you have the right objectives when you are attempting to communicate, the first step is already completed. In other words, you are halfway there.

There are 20 steps for excellent speech preparation.

Basic Speech Categories

1. **To Entertain**
2. **To Inform**
3. **To Inspire**
4. **To Convince**
5. **To Persuade**

Once the purpose of the speech has been determined, then you can begin to plan and arrange your talk to support the central theme. In this section we are going to work on all five types of speeches, under a little different type of heading, but the same types nevertheless.

To get started, ask yourself these twenty questions. The answers (written below each question) will help you with the preparation of any type of presentation. The answers are basic. They do not change. Learn them, adapt them into your personal style, and become the success you have the right to be.

20 Steps for Excellent Preparation

1. What used to be your excuse for not doing public speaking?

    a. Stage fright.

    b. Never done it before.

    c. Don't know what to talk about.

    d. Might forget.

    e. Don't know how to put a speech together.

    f. Don't have anything to say.

    g. What if they ask questions?

2. What are some of the benefits to you of public speaking?

    a. Become a better conversationalist.

    b. Become a more interesting person.

    c. Become more self-confident.

    d. Become more creative.

    e. Improve thinking and reasoning abilities.

    f. Improve vocabulary.

    g. Improve reading and listening skills.

    h. Help handle criticism.

    i. Helps you stand out in a crowd.

3. Does stage fright work for you or against you?

It can work for you if you can control your nervousness. When your adrenaline is pumping a little extra hard, it will make your mind sharper and give you the excitement in your attitude and voice that excites others. The key is to learn how to make your nervousness work for you and not against you. (We will talk more about this later.)

4. How does one get started in public speaking?

Plan to speak every time you get an opportunity. It will help you develop your skills and make people aware of your talents and abilities. Where can you get an opportunity to speak?

a. Accept speaking assignments, like oral reports or presentations at work.

b. Volunteer to become an officer in an organization, and you will usually have an opportunity to make a brief report at the meetings.

c. Civic organizations are always looking for speakers. Offer your services in an area of your expertise. It might be a subject related to your job or maybe one related to one of your hobbies.

d. Political and labor organizations offer a variety of speaking opportunities.

e. Teaching or making presentations in a religious atmosphere or within a study group or committee will provide additional opportunities.

f. Become active in groups such as scouts, garden clubs, Chamber of Commerce, school parent organizations, children's sport organizations, hobby clubs, book clubs, etc. The list is endless.

g. Step out and offer your services whenever and wherever the opportunity arises. Don't be afraid, and don't get in a rut. No one is going to put you down for giving your best. Most audiences will pull for you if you have prepared and are giving it your all.

5. How much preparation should you do for each minute at the lectern?

You will need about one hour of preparation for each minute you spend at the lectern. No, I did not make a mistake; I said *one hour for every one minute.*

6. What should you consider when you choose a subject?

a. Talk about something that you care about.

b. Believe in what you are saying.

c. Talk to the interest of your audience.

d. Give the audience something to take home with them.

7. Where do you find good speech material?

a. Become a good listener. You will hear topics in conversations, on the radio or TV, in meetings, at clubs, at church, from your family and friends.

b. Be an avid reader. You will find topics in books, newspapers, journals, manuals, magazines, and even in your e-mails.

c. Become familiar with the public libraries and your own library, and keep articles on file that you find interesting. They are a wonderful source of quick ideas.

8. Your credibility as a speaker depends upon what?

Being honest with all materials that you use will go a long way toward assuring your credibility. If you use a quote, offer it as such; if you are paraphrasing, then acknowledge that as well. Be sure that your material is accurate. Verify your sources. The Internet has great availability in that area. Keep your facts straight. If you are not sure about a statistic, don't use it.

9. What are the three main sections of a speech? Briefly describe the importance of each.

a. The Beginning:

This is the part of your speech that catches their attention. If you are not able to do that in the very beginning, you will never have your audience with you. It should be dynamic, maybe shocking, maybe dramatic, but at least attention getting. Memorize it, as it must be exact.

b. The Middle:

This is your story. It is the area that flows from A – B – C in a logical and smooth manner. It is the part where you deliver the core of the idea in your presentation. It should be told, not read. If absolutely necessary, an outline may be used for sequencing, but, please, do not read to the audience. They are usually quite capable of reading for themselves and did not come to hear you read to them.

c. The End:

This is the statement that will be remembered. It must be clear, clean, and concise. It, as with the beginning, must be memorized because it must be exact if you want the ideas to be carried away.

You will need about one hour of preparation for each minute you spend at the lectern.

10. **a. Should you personally use humor?**

Are you funny? Can you tell a joke to your friends and get a laugh? If you can, then perhaps you can use tasteful humor. If not, this is not the place to try.

b. How is humor used correctly?

Humor can be used very effectively to make a point or to make a point more memorable. However, it must never be cruel, cause someone to suffer, or be crude.

11. **What types of visual aids are available?**

There are so many technical advances coming into play each and every day that the type and selection of visual aids is limited only to your ability to use what is available to your company and to you personally. We have films, CDs, power points, YouTube, opaque projectors, overhead projectors, workbooks, handouts, displays, story boards, e-books, Kindles, and the selection goes on and on. Use what you are most comfortable with and what presents your ideas in the most effective and efficient manner. Do keep in mind, however, the manner in which people receive ideas—aurally, visually and kinesthetically. Know your audience and be willing to do what it takes to reach each of them.

12. There are 3 ways to deliver a presentation. What are they?

Technically, there are three ways to deliver a presentation: memorized, read, or impromptu/extemporaneous. I totally object. Any presentation that is memorized or read is, almost without exception, boring. People who are accustomed to giving presentations can give impromptu or extemporaneous speeches with reasonable skill, because of their experience. It is not a great idea for a novice. Refer back to question Number 9 for the most effective techniques for a memorable speech.

Any presentation that is memorized or read is, almost without exception, boring.

13. Name 5 reasons why you never make a presentation without practice.

    a. Correct speech: grammar, sentence structure, word use, etc.

    b. Logical organization.

    c. Adequate information—not overdone or underdone.

    d. Good use of visuals.

    e. Timing.

14. Name 5 things you do just before your presentation.

a. Meet the person who is introducing you and give them a brief outline of information for your introduction.

b. If handouts are being used, arrange for someone to assist you with them.

c. Check the room and the equipment that you will be using to make sure that it is suitable and working properly.

d. Meet as many people in your audience as possible.

e. Take a few minutes just before the presentation for yourself—focus, concentrate, give yourself a pep talk, and quickly review your speech.

15. Become aware of your appearance, your voice, and your mannerisms when you are making a presentation.

Many skills have been discussed in this book as well as interview techniques and professional appearance. They all apply here. If you have some questions as to how you should look or behave, check back in that particular section and do a quick review.

16. How do you develop a pleasant speaking style?

a. Be yourself. Always be a first-rate you. Never try to speak or act like someone else. Learn from their traits, but just be the best you that you can be.

b. Be enthusiastic. It is contagious. If you are excited about your subject, chances are your audience will become excited, too. The audience has a tendency to follow your lead.

c. Be sincere. Will Rogers was sincere when he said, "I never met a man I didn't like." His audiences understood. Nothing replaces sincerity.

17. How do you handle unexpected disturbances?

a. Unexpected noise. If you stop and look in the direction of the noise, so will your audience. They will follow your lead. If you don't react and continue, they will continue with you.

b. The drunk or heckler. First of all, remember that they are not as prevalent as you might think. In all the years I spent on the lecture circuit, I had one heckler and never had a drunk accost me, although I did make a presentation one evening to a very drunk audience. They were very quiet because most of them were asleep. They had already had their cocktail hour and their dinner and were feeling no pain. The key in both cases is to remain calm and keep your poise. Remember, the audience will almost always follow your lead.

c. Mistakes. Inevitably at some point during your speaking years, you will do or say something that you have no idea where it came from. If at all possible, just ignore it and continue with your talk. In that case, the audience will either think that they misunderstood what you said or that it didn't happen at all. Sometimes, it is not a word or action that gets off key, it may be that your papers get hit by a fan and fly off across the room or the lectern collapses or the lights go out. If it can happen, at some point it will. If you can collect a few spontaneous remarks to cover those accidents, they will save your day and may become the highlight of your entire speech.

18. If during a question and answer session you are asked a question to which you do not know the answer, what do you say?

Be yourself! Always be a first-rate you.

Always be honest, and *never* fake an answer. If you do not know the answer, simply say, "That is a good question. I do not know the answer, but I will be happy to check on it and get back to you."

19. How do you evaluate your presentation?

I am my own best critic. I know how to evaluate my presentations and how to handle the challenges. (We will talk about this technique a little later.) As long as I continue to make presentations, I will periodically record them, both visually and orally. That way I can readjust anything that has slipped into my presentation style and does not need to be there. It can also be very helpful for your ego.

The evening of the bosses' night presentation when everyone was "asleep," I happen to have taped my talk. I was pretty down, as the applause following my presentation was very slim. I have never been so glad to have a tape in my life because I popped it into my car tape player on the way home, and I am here to tell you, I made one dynamite speech that night. They blew it! They probably missed one of the best speeches of their lives.

20. What is the main key to any successful presentation?

There is one key, and it covers all topics—thorough preparation.

H.E.L.P.

Go to www.howtogetandkeepajob.com for free work pages:
Worksheet for 20 basic questions

Notes

CHAPTER 14
Let's Go to Work!

If I talk, will you hear me? If you hear, are you listening?
If you are listening, will you understand?
If you understand, will you care?

Author unknown

How to Get Started

Excuses are a dime a dozen. If you want one, there is always one available. Sometimes we give ourselves excuses that we are too old or too young or it is too late or there is really no reason to learn another skill at this point in life. Bosh! All of those things are not reasons, they are just excuses. If you want to be on the cutting edge of your career, if you aspire to go to the top, if you want to make life better and easier for yourself and your family, then you have to stretch and grow.

SO…let's throw all the excuses out of the window and go to work.

Get a Camera

There are many places where you can take classes on public speaking. There are also a multitude of books, but you can take all of the available classes and read all of the books, and if you don't get up and start speaking, it won't happen. For most of us, time is of the essence, so what I am going to do in the next four chapters is share a technique that you can use at home, in private and in your free time, to help you get started on your public speaking skills.

When you can make the time, I strongly suggest that you join a group called Toastmasters International. They, as their name says, are all over the world and are a group of people who are interested in improving their skills in a positive environment.

As a member you will go through a series of speeches and will receive evaluations on each of your presentations so that you may learn and grow. *However*, the evaluations will *only be positive*. You will never be criticized or put down in any way. I was a member for many years and learned so much from them. They were a wonderful support group for the growth that I was trying to accomplish.

In the meantime, get a camera. Why? Because you need to see what you are doing when you practice speaking. If you don't have one, beg, borrow, or steal one. (Just kidding, don't steal one—have a garage sale and go buy one.) It doesn't have to be fancy, just useable. While you are working through the next four chapters, you will be using it a lot. Each time you make a presentation, you need to record it and then, as you will be instructed, look at it and evaluate your skills. No, you don't have to show it to anyone else and, no, you don't have to record every speech you make. However, it is very wise to periodically record and/or video your future presentations. If you want to grow and learn, you need to know what you are doing. Recordings are very revealing.

As we talked earlier, there are many types of speeches. For our purpose, we are going to be working on four. This will give you an overview of techniques which may be used as a basis for building other types of presentations.

4 Speech Projects

We are going to be working on these four types of speeches:

"I" Story: This is by far the easiest type of speech to make because it is about you, and who knows your story better than you?

What I Love To Do: This speech will help you learn to describe an activity or process so that others can visualize or comprehend your thoughts.

Show and Tell: In this presentation you will begin handling items as you speak. It could be anything from a toothbrush to a workbook.

Convince Me: Now it is time to begin working on persuasion and techniques that will help you put all of the above ideas into a workable format.

While you are working on each of these speech projects, you will also be learning skills such as how to connect with your audience, how to control your hands and body when speaking, how to use visuals, and how to handle verbal blunders.

You will be asked to prepare each speech in a specific manner. There will be special new skills added to each presentation. Once you have the material prepared and have practiced sufficiently (not forever), then you will record your own presentation. At the end of each chapter, there will be an evaluation form for your personal use as you watch the recorded program. You will also receive specific instructions about how to evaluate yourself and how to motivate yourself. Yes, there are a lot of things to learn, but if you will accept the fact that you never will be perfect, then you will be okay. You are and always will be learning. I have given hundreds of speeches, and I still learn from every one of them.

You are and always will be learning.

One bit of advice before we get started—don't be afraid of your audience. Almost without exception, audiences are your friends. They feel with you and want you to succeed. The only exception is if you come to them obviously unprepared. That is an insult, and they will recognize it and will not appreciate it. As we discussed earlier, be excellent. Give it all you have to give each and every time you speak. There is nothing more that an audience can ask of you, and they will love you for it.

H.E.L.P.

Go to www.howtogetandkeepajob.com for free work pages:
Sample speaking engagements
Sample speaking topics

Notes

CHAPTER 15
Practice Speech No. 1

The invitation – the great honor.

Author unknown

The "I" Story

What is an "I" Story? It is the story about you. It is the easiest presentation that you will ever give because you have all of the research material right there in your brain...you lived it. No one can criticize your information, deny the truthfulness of it (if you are truthful), or prepare it any better than you. You are this story.

This is a sample "I" Story:

"I am a born and bred Okie. My name is Donna Watson, and I am a wife, mother, teacher, author, and professional speaker. I was born in western Oklahoma more years ago than I prefer to share with you. My family is from that part of the country as well, and my husband's parents and mine went to high school together in Cordell, Oklahoma. That is how we met. Actually, our mothers are the ones who decided that we should get married. They have good taste.

"My husband, Robert, and I have two daughters, a son-in-law, and three grandsons and, of course, they are the most beautiful, handsome, and talented children in the entire world. We both have doctorate degrees and have pursued our respective professions while raising our children. Our goal is to have a strong Christian family and to be able to serve our community well.

"As we are now partially retired, we would like to do more traveling, but since we adopted a puppy in a brain-dead moment, that is not as easy as it might have been. Having a new puppy is like having a new baby in the house. If we didn't love her so much, we would change our minds. But, she is here to stay.

"I have many, many hobbies and interests. I, of course, love to read and write. My husband says I *used* to be an artist. He says that because I never seem to find time to paint any more. I sew for a children's program I helped to create and for the preemie baby program that I now coordinate. I am very active in my community because this is my season to give back to the people who have given so much to us.

"You see, I love living in America. I love living in Oklahoma. Why? Because I am a born and bred Okie."

That speech took 1 minute and 36 seconds to present. I am not asking you to speak forever, even if it does seem like it. I am asking you to begin.

Let's look at this speech. What do you see that is exaggerated and repeated? The beginning and end, of course. I did that specifically because I want you to never forget how important those two parts of a speech are.

The first sentence of your speech grabs the audience. The last one is what they will remember and the middle is the story.

The first sentence is the one that grabs you. If you do not connect with your audience in those first few moments, you never will. It needs to be something unusual: it might be a bold statistic, a dramatic movement, a shocking thought, or something that is out of character for you personally. For me, this was out of character. Most people who know me and know that I am a professional speaker, know that I don't usually use local lingo when I am speaking. I would not normally refer to myself as an "Okie." I did that on purpose to make it memorable.

The final statement is the one that will be remembered. If you ask someone what a speaker talked about, they will generally recap the final statement. If you want to make a point in your speech, it must be either made or reiterated in the last statement. The first and last statements are not normally the same. They can be, as they were in my speech, but it is unusual. I did that on purpose to make you very aware of those two elements.

The beginning and ending statements must be carefully constructed and memorized. You do not want to mess up those two statements. If the rest of your speech falls apart and you have successfully presented those two statements, then you will be okay.

The middle of the presentation is your story. This applies whether you are telling an "I" Story or whether you are presenting a proposal to your client. The information is more meaningful and believable if it is told in sequence and in a conversational tone. You have prepared this information, and you know the material; therefore, it should never be a challenge to share it with others.

If you have a great deal of information to share, it is permissible to use an outline, but *never* a written speech. I have, on occasion, written out a speech and then highlighted the important parts and taken the highlighted outline with me. This may be necessary if you are presenting technical material and must be very sure that your statistics are accurate.

Another way to use an outline is to have it on a screen or in a handout so that the audience can follow along with you. We will talk more about visual aids later.

Take a Break

Take a break now and prepare your "I" speech. Give yourself about three minutes to put your ideas together. Use a timer. You do not need all day. Postponing the actual speech is just another excuse, and we are through with excuses.

This speech does not require a research project, so simply think about the topics you want to cover, the order in which you want to cover them, and any special anecdote you might want to share. This will not take much of your three minutes. Spend the rest of your three minutes writing a specific beginning and ending statement and memorizing them.

Okay, you are ready. Set up your new camera, stand up in front of it and turn it on (or have someone do it for you if you choose). Yes, I said "stand up." We rarely give speeches sitting down. You may give some presentations to your clients/ customers while sitting, but I think you will find that if you can manage to stand for a presentation, it will be more dynamic and full of energy.

Record your "I" Story.

Don't watch it!

How to Self-Evaluate

Before you turn on the video to watch your first presentation, take the evaluation sheet from the end of this chapter, get a pen, and get ready to take notes.

Watch for three things:

1. Your beginning sentence. How did it come across? Would it have attracted someone's attention if they had not been ready for your talk? Would it have made them look up and think that maybe this speaker is worth listening to?

2. Make a list and count the number of times you said, "uh," "ah," "well," "like," and "you know." Are there any other words that you tend to use repetitively? Don't get upset. This is a normal speech pattern for those who are untrained speakers. We do this because we need to think. Instead of just remaining silent for a moment and allowing our brains to work, we feel the need to fill the silence.

A simple pause is much more powerful. The pause not only gives you time to think, but it also gives your audience time to catch up with your thoughts and makes them aware that this particular thought is worth remembering.

Paul Harvey was a news commentator for many years. He is gone now, but if you can find a recording of any of his speeches, get it and listen carefully. He was a master at what is called the "pregnant pause." He not only used them for his benefit but in a way that produced a powerful point without having to say so.

A simple pause is much more powerful than an "uh."

From this point on, you need to become aware of the words that you are using to fill a need for a pause even in your everyday conversations. Think about it as you talk until a mental "red flag" pops up every time you use one of those "fill-in" words and you can learn to eliminate them from your general manner of speaking.

3. The ending sentence. This is the second-most important statement you will make in your presentation. I would say that it is the most important, because it is where you will make your point. However, if you do not catch the audience's attention in the first sentence, they are not going to hear the last one. As a result, the ending sentence must be carefully worded. It must be powerful and it must be a summary of what you want remembered. And, you must memorize it. If you blow this statement, you have blown the speech.

Now you may watch your recording.

Applaud! Yell! Whistle! Do whatever you choose to make a very big deal out of what you have just accomplished. It is a big deal!

This is important. When was the last time you had a round of applause? High School? Earlier? Well, that is too long. It is time. You need to do this out loud and often so that you can begin to hear the applause in your head. Then when you are making a presentation to a client/customer, you can give yourself that needed silent applause on the way out of the door. You may not always give the presentation that you wish you had, but if you gave it your best, if you did the best job that you could that day, in that set of circumstances, with that information and with that amount of skill, you were excellent, and you need and deserve a round of applause.

Never forget: you are good. You are special.

Save this recording, and let's move on to No. 2. **Yes, I said save it.**

Applaud! Yell! Whistle! Celebrate!

H.E.L.P.

Go to www.howtogetandkeepajob.com for free work pages:
Evaluation Form No. 1

Your Evaluation Form

Practice Speech No. 1

The "I" Story

Date recorded: _____

Beginning statement: _____

_____

Did you memorize it? _____ Would it have drawn attention to your speech? _____

How could you improve your beginning statement? _____

Rewrite your beginning statement: _____

_____

Was the middle of your speech sequential? _____

How could it be improved? _____

Count your repetitive words:

"Uh"_____   "Ah"_____   "Well"_____

"Like"_____   "You know"_____   Other words_____

Ending Statement: _____

_____

Did you memorize it? _____

Was your ending statement a memorable conclusion? _____

How could you improve it? _____

Rewrite your ending statement: _____

_____

Did you applaud? _____ **You should have!!!**

Notes

CHAPTER 16
Practice Speech No. 2

Nothing in life is to be feared. It is only to be understood.

Marie Curie

The "What I Love To Do" Speech

As we progress through this series of speeches, you will be adding speaking techniques to your repertoire. In speech No. 1, you learned how to stand and speak before a camera, how to put a speech together, and the importance of being aware of fill-in phrases to cover up your pauses. In this speech we are going to work on hand and body movements and how to work with your audience.

Preparing the Speech

First, let's put the speech together. The topic this time is "What I Love To Do" and that is exactly what it is all about. The topic can be anything that you love to do from brushing your teeth to skiing down a mountain. You may wish to explain how to fold up a parachute or do parallel parking. It does not matter as long as you love to do it.

Practice! Practice! Practice!

Set the speech up as usual: Create and memorize your beginning sentence.

In the middle you will sequentially share the information about how and why you love this particular topic.

1. Describe it.

2. Explain how to accomplish it.

3. Describe the benefits of doing this.

4. Encourage others to enjoy the benefits of your choice.

The ending sentence must be memorable. Summarize the topic and its benefits in a manner that will be unique and interesting. Memorize it.

Practice – Practice – Practice

We are getting into a little different element of speaking now, and it does take preparation. Your goal for this speech should be approximately three minutes, which means that it will probably take about three hours of preparation and practice for you to be ready to present in an excellent manner. Don't rush it. You are on a learning curve, and as you add each step and new technique, it will take time to absorb and become comfortable with them. That is okay.

Once you have your speech information prepared, begin to practice. I have found that practicing in front of a mirror is always very helpful. It was especially helpful when I was learning how to effectively use my body language. There are several segments that you will want to work on all at once—your eyes, your hands, your feet, your posture, and your movement are just a few of them.

Body Language

Eyes

As we discussed earlier, the eyes are a very powerful form of communication. It is important that you have eye contact with your audience if you want them to continue paying attention to you and your presentation. If, as it is for many people, it is too uncomfortable for you to look at their eye (remember, you can't look at both at the same time), then look at their forehead. From the lectern, an audience cannot usually tell the difference. Look around the room and try to cover all areas. People don't want to be left out by a speaker. Basically what you are telling them is: "I am speaking to you because I care about you and I have something important to share."

If, during this time, you can comfortably call someone by name in your audience, it will make the entire audience sit up and take notice. When you first came in, you were hopefully able to meet a number of your audience members. Try to remember at least a first name or two and approximately what part of the room they are sitting in. If you look in the right-hand corner of the room and talk to Tom, and he happens not to be there, it is okay. Most likely the rest of the audience doesn't know Tom anyway, and they just assume that you know someone that they do not. Referring to people by name is another way of letting people know that they are important to you.

Hands

Your hands are very revealing. If you are wringing them or squeezing them or treating them like they are some element from outer space that you don't know what to do with, then that, too, is what your audience will concentrate on.

Keep them still. Leave them comfortably at your side or gently on the lectern. "Gently" means that you do not grip the lectern so tightly that you are showing white knuckles. Keeping them at your side will prevent what is referred to as the "crotch salute" or the "fig leaf" stance. A very popular e-mail in recent years was of a picture of President Obama exhibiting the "crotch salute" during the national anthem that was being played in Indianola, Iowa. Everyone else was saluting the American flag, and apparently he was not aware that was happening or of what he was doing with his hands. It is not generally an action that your audience will forget.

If you are comfortable gesturing to make a point, then do so, but be careful how you gesture. People who are nervous have a tendency to glue their arms to their sides and wave from the elbows out. Yes, this does look rather awkward. This is another reason to practice in front of the mirror.

Don't point. Pointing is what your mother does when you are in trouble. Your audience does not want to be lectured to. Instead, gesture with an open hand. A turned-down hand is a sign of a put-down or can be used for a negative point as opposed to the open hand, which is an invitation to listen and become involved.

Posture

Please, stand up straight. Do not slump or lean on the lectern. Keep your feet slightly apart for stability and bend your knees very slightly as is done in the military or in a band that is standing at attention for a long period of time. This gives you a more comfortable and relaxed look, and if you look comfortable and relaxed, your audience will become so. You are their leader.

Swinging from side to side or front to back is what children do in the yard. It is not what speakers do during a presentation. They are not watching a tennis match, so don't make them dizzy. It is okay to move, of course. In fact, some movement helps you be more comfortable and can, in turn, relax the audience, but don't pace. It will take them right back to that tennis match, and your audience will spend more time going back and forth, back and forth, than they will listening to what you have to say.

Presentation

Are you ready? Have you written and memorized your opening and closing sentences? Are they memorable? Is the body of your presentation in a comfortable sequence? Have you practiced, and practiced, and practiced?

Okay, **record.**

Don't watch it.

Always Evaluate

Get the evaluation sheet at the end of the chapter, find a comfy chair, a good pen and, when you are all ready, **watch your recording**.

Watch the entire video before doing your evaluation, or you will miss something. You may even need to watch it again as you begin to do the evaluation, *but right now*, at the end of the first viewing, **Applaud! Yell! Tell yourself how wonderful you are, because you are!**

You are the best friend that you have. Encourage yourself, your efforts and your talents. You are good!!

Listen to the applause. Close your eyes and absorb the sound of the applause so that you will eventually be able to hear it in your mind. This is more important than you know. **You are the best friend that you have.** Be that good friend and support yourself and your efforts and your talents. **You are good!**

Now that you have watched your presentation, carefully go through the evaluation and then try a new technique—self-evaluation.

The Sandwich Evaluation

I told you earlier that I am the best critic I have because I know how to evaluate myself. I want you to learn that technique, too, because if you are like most people, the first thing you started to do when you watched that video was to beat yourself up for what you **did not** do. Wrong!

The Sandwich Evaluation is a technique whereby you look at what you have accomplished and 1) recognize the thing that you did best, 2) recognize *the* item that you need to work on at this point (please note that I said, "the" not "those"), 3) recognize what you are repeatedly doing best. Write these down on your evaluation sheet and reread them again and again.

Remember when we talked about affirmations and visualization in Chapter 5? This is the time to apply them. Turn your positive points into affirmations. For example, let's say that you did not use a lot of repetitive language in this presentation. You might write this affirmation: "My language is clean, clear, and concise when I am speaking."

As we also learned in that skill study, it is important to repeat affirmations over and over again and out loud. What this will do is reinforce what you are doing **right** and will program your mind to repeat that action. As you give more and more speeches and add more and more "right" actions to your list, your "negative" list or "need to improve" list will become increasingly smaller.

Congratulations! You Are On Your Way!

H.E.L.P.

Go to www.howtogetandkeepajob.com for free work pages:
Evaluation Form No. 2

Your Evaluation Form

Practice Speech No. 2

The "What I Love To Do" Speech

Date recorded: _____

Speech Title: _____

What is your subject? _____

How long did you take to prepare this three-minute speech? _____

What was your beginning statement? _____

_____

Did you memorize it? _____ If you were not pleased with your beginning

statement, rewrite it: _____

_____

Observe your body language:

    Did you look at the entire audience? _____

    Did you call anyone by name? _____

    Did your hands look comfortable? _____

    Were you able to use them smoothly? _____

    Did you stand up straight? _____

    Did you avoid swinging or pacing? _____

What was your ending statement? _____

_____

Did you memorize it? _____ If you were not pleased with your ending

statement, rewrite it: _____

Did you applaud? Yell? Tell yourself how good you are becoming? You should!

Sandwich Evaluation:

What was the *best* thing you did during this presentation: _____

_____

Name *one* thing you need to work on at this time: _____

_____

What did you do both times that you feel really good about? _____

_____

Don't Stop! Keep Growing!

CHAPTER 17
Practice Speech No. 3

Keep in mind what you have to do when you are afraid.
If you are prepared you will not be afraid.

Dale Carnegie

The "Show and Tell" Speech

As with speeches No. 1 and No. 2, the first thing to do to prepare for this speech is to choose a topic. In this case, it has to be an object, as you are going to learn how to handle items as you speak. It should be something that you can have fun with, explain, or show how it functions. The more you can work with it, the easier your speech will be.

This is your introduction into the use of visual aids. Still having trouble figuring out what to do with your hands? We just solved your dilemma. Anytime you are using visual aids, your hands are busy, and you don't have to worry about where to put them.

Types of Visual Aids

There are as many types of visual aids as you have ideas. They can range from electronic equipment to a child's toy. In other words, the visual aid is whatever you need to explain the purpose of your presentation.

Visual aids are powerful tools for effective communication.

Visual aids are powerful tools for effective communication. Use them every chance you have as they will increase the understanding of the ideas presented—

especially to visual people. They will also save time, enhance attention, and help you control your nervousness.

Basic Rules for Visual Aid Use

You will choose your visual aids based on several considerations:

1. What message are you trying to convey?
2. How large is your audience?
3. How is the meeting room designed?
4. What equipment is available?
5. How much preparation time do you have?
6. What can you afford?

If you choose to use electronic equipment, remember that you are responsible for checking it and making sure that it is in working condition. Also, be sure that extra light bulbs, electric cords, etc. are available in case of an emergency. Be prepared for any type of disaster. As you know, if it can happen it will; bulbs burn out, power goes out, coffee is spilled on your handouts, your notes blow off the lectern and are scattered across the room. (By the way, if you have any type of notes, it is mandatory that they be sequentially numbered so if they are dropped or blow away, you can put them back together in a minimum amount of time.)

Location and Size of Your Visuals

If you are projecting an image on any type of screen, *never* leave it blank. A huge white space on a screen or wall will immediately draw the attention of your audience, and you have lost them. Be sure that screens are located where everyone can easily see what you are sharing, and if you are using a handheld item, be very careful about its size. If the audience is small, a small item may work fine, but a matchbook in a room of four or five-hundred people will be lost.

Where you hold your visual is also very important. Again, the size of your audience is of utmost importance. If you have a small audience, you can hold the item in front of you or out for them to observe. If you are looking at a larger audience, the item must be held high enough for the ones at the rear of the seating area to observe as well as those on the front row.

The same rule is true with hand motions. If I were to hold up three fingers when you and I are talking, you could see them just fine. If I held them up at the same location in the front of my body when the room is packed, you still might be the only one who could see them. In that case, my hand would need to be above my head.

A Few More Quick Ideas

1. **Introduce the visual before using it.**

2. **If you are using a workbook and need to turn the page, make an obvious turn so that the audience will follow your lead.**

3. **Avoid visuals with numbers as they are hard to read.**

4. **Explain what you are showing for those who are aural. They won't be looking at it.**

5. **Do not talk with your back to the audience. If you are using a whiteboard and cannot write sideways, then wait until you finish writing before speaking.**

6. **Use explanatory titles rather than "Chart 1."**

7. **Do not overuse visuals. You do not need one for every point.**

8. **Rehearse! It may not be as easy to use visuals as it appears to be. As with everything that has to do with speaking—rehearse.**

Using a Microphone

Please, do not ever say, "Oh no, I do not need to use a microphone. I have a very strong voice, and everyone will be able to hear me." That is such a copout. In the first place, you cannot guarantee that everyone in the room hears as well as you, and in second place, saying that you do not need a mike (microphone) in a room where one is offered simply says that you are afraid to use it.

If a microphone is available – use it!

For this presentation practice, try to borrow a lapel mike. A free-standing mike is harder to use, and unless it is attached to the lectern, is not usually available. If you have a head attachment, the challenges of using a mike are somewhat eliminated.

The free-standing mike is a challenge because if you turn away from it, you will lose your volume. Therefore, you must stand very still and primarily hold your head in one position. It is very limiting.

The lapel mike is the one that people seem to have the most challenges with. If they are not accustomed to using a mike, they will tend to put it somewhere in the area of their stomach. No one wants to hear your stomach growl. We want to hear your voice, so put the mike where that happens. It should be, for a man, located right under the knot of his tie, and for a woman, as close to the same location as possible. If you wear it on the lapel, you will have the same challenges as for a free-standing mike. If you turn your head the other way, you will lose your volume.

The head attachment moves with you and is usually cord free. It is, by all means, the preferred means of using voice projection equipment.

Test your mike before your presentation, and have someone walk to the back and sides of the room to see if they can hear clearly. What may seem too loud for you may be just right for those sitting farther away.

How to Motivate Yourself

You have now reached the level of speaking that requires you to be responsible for yourself at all levels. You need to be able to prepare yourself, motivate yourself, praise yourself, and evaluate yourself. The whole package is yours, and if you have taken these lessons step by step, you are ready.

A little bit of nervousness or "extra energy" is what puts you on the cutting edge. It gives you the sharpness to attract and hold the attention of your audience.

It is important to be excited about what you are going to share. If you are not overly excited, the audience will never get just a little bit excited. I always feel as though I have to be functioning about two feet off the floor for me to wake up my audience. How do I do that?

I start preparing when I leave home or leave my hotel room. On the way to the speaking center, I say to myself over and over again, out loud if possible, "I am the best. I am the best. I am the best."

By now you should recognize that as an affirmation that I am using to program my subconscious mind to help me give the best presentation that I am capable of giving at that particular time on that particular day. *If* I do not feel a slight adrenaline rush by the time I get to the area where I am speaking, then I try to find some place private where I can jump up and down for a moment or two. A higher than normal level of adrenaline, or extra energy, is required to give an excellent presentation. If I have traveled all night the night before or have been sick and had very little rest, I have to work at getting the extra energy. This "extra energy," as I choose to call it, is what you may identify as nervousness. I do not use that word, as it has negative connotations for me. It is just like the word "problem" that we discussed in an earlier skill. Why would I want to be nervous, you might ask? That little bit of nervousness or "extra energy" is what puts me on the cutting edge. It gives me the sharpness to attract and hold the attention of an audience that I could not get any other way.

Preparing Your Presentation

The basic preparation of this speech is the same as the others—a beginning, a middle, and an end. One new skill I would like for you to add is that when you make your closing statement, be very, very careful that you say nothing afterwards. The closing sentence is designed to leave an impression or an idea or a thought with your audience, one that you would like for them to remember. If you say something afterwards, that impression, idea, or thought is negated just as if you had said, "but" or "however" before your next statement.

For example, let's say that you had just made a dynamic talk about the dangers of having squirrels around your home. Your ending statement, made in a dramatic and precisely enunciated manner, was, "Squirrels can destroy your home." Will that stay with them? Yes, it will. If, however, you had said, "Squirrels can destroy your home. But they are so cute." What would that have done to your dynamic close, and what would your audience have most likely remembered? Do you think they are really going to leave there thinking about how dangerous squirrels can be, or are they going to leave thinking about how cute they are?

As you are putting the final touches on this presentation and beginning to *practice*, remember to incorporate all of the techniques that we have included in the last two chapters:

1. Dynamic beginning
2. Repetitive language

3. Pregnant pauses

4. Body language

    a. Eyes

    b. Hands

    c. Posture

5. Use of visual aids

6. Use of a microphone

7. Self-motivation

8. Memorable close

9. Silence

10. Hearing applause in your mind

11. Sandwich evaluation

This presentation should also be about three minutes long, so now that you have studied your skills and spent three hours preparing and practicing:

Record the speech

Applaud in your mind

Watch the recording

Complete the evaluation

You Are Almost There And Getting Better Every Time!

H.E.L.P.

Go to www.howtogetandkeepajob.com for free work pages:
Evaluation Form No. 3

Your Evaluation Form

Practice Speech No. 3

The "Show and Tell" Speech

Date recorded: _____

Speech Title: _____

What is your subject? _____

How long did you take to prepare this three-minute speech? _____

What was your beginning statement: _____

_____

Did you memorize it? _____ If you were not pleased with your beginning

statement, rewrite it: _____

_____

What type of visual aid(s) did you use? _____

Were you comfortable using it (them)? _____

How could you have used them more effectively? _____

_____

Was there another item that would have improved your connection with your

audience?_____ What was it and how would it have made your speech better?

_____

Did you use a mike? _____ What type? _____ What can you

do to become more comfortable with a mike and make it work for you? _____

_____

How did you motive yourself to control your "excess energy"?_____

Did you use repetitive words? _____ If so, which word(s) do you need to work

on? _____ Are you beginning to use pregnant pauses? _____

How was your body language? Eyes: _____ Hands:_____

Posture:_____ Movement: _____

What was your ending statement? _____

_____

Did you memorize it? _____ If you were not pleased with your ending

statement, rewrite it: _____

_____

Did you remain silent after your ending statement? _____

Did you hear applause in your mind? _____

Sandwich Evaluation:

What was the *best* thing you did during this presentation? _____

_____

Name *one* thing you need to work on at this time: _____

What are you doing each time that you feel really good about? _____

Were you EXCELLENT?
You are capable of being EXCELLENT every time!

Notes

CHAPTER 18
Practice Speech No. 4

The best orator is one who can
make men see with their ears.

Arab proverb

The "Convince Me" Speech

The "Convince Me" speech is the art of persuasion. It is used a lot in business. The other speeches you have been working on are the stepping stones to this key presentation.

As you are preparing this speech, it is important to do your research very carefully. Whether you are presenting to a client/customer or to a conference, the accuracy of statistics and knowledge is essential to your good reputation. Don't fake it. Become believable and sincere, or you will lose the confidence of your client/customer and never have a chance to complete your contract with them.

An excellent presentation puts you on the cutting edge in a competitive market.

This is where you will need to apply all the skills that you have learned in this book—at the same time: read your audience, treat them in the manner in which you prefer to be treated, sincerely care about them, honor their time schedules, be sure that your word is good, and present your ideas through the best of your presentation skills. This is the cutting edge. This is what takes people to the top in their fields. This is what makes them excellent, every day.

How to Handle Questions

Before any presentation to a client/customer or to a group where you will be handling a question and answer session, think carefully through all of your material and write out a series of questions or challenges that someone might present to you about your topic. Ask yourself or have someone else ask you the hardest questions that you can come up with. Because you know your material so well, it is most likely that you will ask yourself much more challenging questions than will the person or persons you will be presenting to. In other words, if you can handle your own questions, the actual questions that you will be handling will usually be a snap.

Never try to pretend you have an answer that you don't really have. It is very easy to see through a bluff. Simply say as we suggested earlier, "That is a very good question. I don't know the answer, but I will be happy to check it out and get back to you." (Then do so.)

Be believable and sincere.

If you are presented with a question that you need to think about for a moment, there are three different ways to handle it:

1. Ask for the question to be repeated.

2. Repeat the question yourself.

3. Pause a moment and give yourself a second to put your thoughts together.

Any one of these three will work to give you the time you need to flip through your mental file and discover the answer that you knew all along.

Prepare Your Presentation

This presentation should be 3 to 5 minutes long as a practice session. After this point your presentations can be of any length depending on the circumstances and the topics. In most instances, you will be given a specific time to speak, and it becomes quite important that you begin to judge time in your mind so that you never take advantage of someone else and their time constraints and/or that you fully fill the time allotted for your presentation.

As you choose your subject and do your research, remember to consider the same steps that we have been building on throughout this section of the book.

16 Steps to an Excellent Presentation

1. **Choose your topic.**

2. **Complete your research.**

3. **Self-motivate for good energy use.**

4. **Design an attention-getting opening.**

5. **Avoid repetitive language.**

6. **Use pregnant pauses.**

7. **Be aware of your body language.**

8. **Use creative visual aids.**

9. **Make good use of your mike.**

10. **Keep body of speech sequential.**

11. **Have a memorable close.**

12. **Remain silent after closing.**

13. **Listen to your mental applause.**

14. **Handle questions with sincerity.**

15. **Complete your sandwich evaluation.**

16. **Celebrate!!**

The time has come. You have prepared, and practiced, and are ready for your final practice presentation, along with a question and answer session, so:

Record the speech.

Applaud in your mind.

Watch the recording.

Evaluate your presentation.

H.E.L.P.

Go to www.howtogetandkeepajob.com for free work pages:
Evaluation Form No. 4

Your Evaluation Form

Practice Speech No. 4

The "Convince Me" Speech

Date recorded: _____

Speech Title: _____

Each time you make a presentation, you should review these 16 topics:

1. What was your topic? _____

2. Did you carefully research your subject? _____

3. Did you use self-motivation to control your energy? _____

4. Did you design and memorize an attention-getting opening? _____

5. Did you avoid repetitive language? _____

6. Did you effectively use pregnant pauses? _____

7. Were you aware of and did you use good body language? _____

8. Did you have creative visual aid(s)? _____

9. Did you made good use of your mike? _____

10. Was the body of your presentation sequential? _____

11. Did you have and memorize a memorable close? _____

12. Did you remain silent after your closing statement? _____

13. Did you hear and listen to your mental applause? _____

14. Did you answer questions honestly and with sincerity? _____

15. Did you complete your sandwich evaluation? _____

16. Did you **Celebrate!?!** _____

And Now...watch your original recording to see how much you have grown.

You are the best!

Life is too short to wake up with regrets.

So love the people who treat you right.

Love the ones who don't, just because you can.

Believe everything happens for a reason.

If you get a second chance, grab it with both hands.

If it changes your life, let it.

Kiss slowly.

Forgive quickly.

God never said life would be easy.

He just promised it would be worth it.

Author unknown

EPILOGUE

Those who hope in the Lord will renew their strength.
They will soar on wings like eagles; they will run and
not grow weary, they will walk and not be faint.

Isaiah 40:31

I had the honor of meeting and hearing Col. Doug Wheelock speak shortly before he became Commander and spent six months at the International Space Station. He shared some very powerful ideas. He reminded us that in every success, there is a group of people who comprise the whole. In that whole group of people, there is not one that is not important. Even if your job seems menial to you, it has a purpose. It is needed to complete the whole.

Never forget that you are important. Never give up on your dreams, and never dream without sharing it with God. Proverbs 16:3 says, "Commit to the Lord whatever you do, and your plans will succeed."

I have shared this article from one of my books with my classes for fifteen years, and I would like to share it with you.

Believe In You

Believe in you because you are unique. You can do things

no one else can do. You can be things no one else can be.

You touch the lives of other people in a way that only you can.

You are a blessing to this world.

You have a right to be here because you are very special.

You are here for an important reason.

Your purpose in this world can be fulfilled by no one else.

Sometimes people and circumstances cause us to doubt our importance.

Please, don't ever let that happen to you.

Believe in you because you have a right to.

If for some reason you can't believe in you right now,

then let me believe in you until you can believe in you.

It would be my privilege.

Chapter One
"101 Simple Ways To Be Good To Yourself"
Donna Watson, Ph.D.

H.E.L.P.

Go to www.howtogetandkeepajob.com for free work pages:
Copy of "Believe In You" suitable for framing.

Share Your Story

Whether you are getting your first job and this book has helped you, or whether you are changing jobs, re-entering the workforce, or simply working toward advancement in your career field, and this book has helped you, please share your success story. Dr. Watson would love to hear from you. You can reach her through her website at

www.howtogetandkeepajob.com.

TIP OF THE DAY

Do you ever wish you had a fresh new idea to give you a boost for the day? Try the "Tip of the Day." Go to **www.howtogetandkeepajob.com** and sign up. It is easy, and it is free! The "Tip of the Day" will come to you each day – Monday through Friday.

Monday – Time Management Tip of the Day

Tuesday – Leadership Tip of the Day

Wednesday – Stress Management Tip of the Day

Thursday - Budgeting Tip of the Day

Friday – "Surprise" Tip of the Day (You really don't want to miss this one! It could be on Goal Setting, Social Media, Recreation, Retirement, Travel, Getting along with Challenging People or maybe just on how to have "Fun!")

Remember, it is FREE and you can sign up by simply going to **www. howtogetandkeepajob.com** and registering today. Remind your friends, too. They could probably use a new idea-booster just as much as the rest of us.

EXTRA

Check the website often for new and fun ideas, such as: calendars full of stress-management tips or leadership tips, E-books and other signature products. You never know what fun, new, and creative ideas you might find. Register at **www.howtogetandkeepajob.com,** and we will keep you posted as new items are produced. They might save you a lot of 'gift shopping' time as well.

Need an **index** for this book? Register at **www.howtogetandkeepajob.com** and find quick references for a more usable text.

Oh yes, we respect you and your privacy—always. Your email address will never be sold or shared. Thank you for trusting us, and we hope that you find great joy in what we have to share.

Is *How to Get and Keep a Job* Designed for You?

How to Get and Keep a Job is designed to help people in many fields. Look through the list below and see if you recognize an area that you might not have thought of. The three sections of this book—How to Get a Job, How to Keep a Job, and How to be on the Competitive Edge—can be used as a total package for self-growth or for group training. They can also be used on an individual basis for skill and advancement training.

Whatever way they would work best for you and your group, we want to help. Please contact Dr. Watson at **www.howtogetandkeepajob.com** to discuss your needs. She can help with seminars, webinars, video training, training materials, leadership training, and even lesson plans. As a professional trainer with many years of experience, she is prepared to help your group reach the level of success that is desired

- **Personal Use**
- **High School Students**
- **Vocational Training Students**
- **College and University Students**
- **Corporate Advancement Training**
- **Not For Profit Organization Programs**
- **Layoff Retraining Programs**
- **Re-entry Training Programs**
- **Military Re-entry Training Programs**
- **Missionary Re-entry Training Programs**
- **And many more…**

There's More!

Visit our website at **www.howtogetandkeepajob.com** and check out all the items that will help in your career challenges. Be sure to come back often for updates on:

Upcoming E-books such as:

- The Importance of Good Self Esteem
- How do I Know Whether I am being Aggressive or Assertive?
- How to Use CCS both Personally and Professionally
-
- Stress Management Calendar
- Stress Test
- Leadership Calendar
- And much, much more!

About the Author

Dr. Donna Watson

Dr. Donna Watson is an internationally known speaker and the best-selling author of several books. An educator, she has enjoyed a forty-year career in training, teaching, and motivational speaking. For fifteen years she taught a course based on the material presented in this book, at Oklahoma Christian University in Edmond, Oklahoma.

The high-energy Watson has spoken to audiences throughout the country on stress management, motivation, leadership, and related topics. She has led seminars and delivered keynote speeches to Fortune 500 executives, government agencies, associations, men and women in towns and cities throughout North America. She is known for her warm and witty style, which encourages people to think, grow, and feel good about themselves. Loving the Lord and praying before each presentation that He will use her as an instrument of His peace and love, has always been her motive.

Dr. Watson holds an undergraduate degree in education and an MBA and PhD in management. Her doctoral dissertation was on stress management.

She is the author of *101 Ways To Enjoy Life's Simple Pleasures* and *101 Simple Ways To Be Good To Yourself*. She has also recorded two albums, *Let Go and Live* on stress and self-esteem, and *Winning Against Stress*, which deals with stress management. As a sideline, while writing her dissertation, she wrote three cookbooks.

Her newest venture, with co-creator Dr. Rita L. Goad, is the *"A Cup of Tea for the Heart"* series. The first book, *"Tough Times Don't Last ~ Tough Women Do"* is full of heartfelt stories and advice from women of faith about the challenges of life and how to live it. Join us for *Joy Thoughts* at teafortheheart.com. You will love them! Watch for new books in this series every year.

Dr. Watson is the co-founder of U R Special Ministries, Inc., a non-profit program that helps at-risk children feel important by providing them with new clothing three times each year. She is also the founder of Baby Luv which is a program that provides miniature quilts for preemie babies at three major hospitals in the Oklahoma City area. She was instrumental in starting the Prayer Power Hotline and weekly church services for The Wellington Retirement Center, where she and her husband, Dr. Robert Watson, taught Bible studies for a number of years.

Dr. Watson and her husband split their time between Branson, Missouri, and Edmond, Oklahoma, where they enjoy time with their daughters and their families. She counts spending time with family and friends, writing, sewing, and painting among her personal simple pleasures.

BIBLIOGRAPHY

Brown, Carla, *Dynamic Communication Skills for Women*, Edited by National Press Publications, Shawnee Mission, Kansas, Communication Series, 1989

DeAngeles, Barbara, *How To Make Love All The Time,* Random House, 1993

Fountain, Elizabeth Haas, *The Polished Professional – How To Put Your Best Foot Forward,* Edited by National Press Publications, Shawnee Mission, Kansas, Communication Series, 1994

Half, Robert, *How To Write A Good Resume,* http://www.nhlink.net/employme/how.htm

Hancuff, Tracy, Vice-President – Wealth Management Advisor, Merrill Lynch, Oklahoma City, OK, 2010

Iles, Robert L., *How To Get the Job You Want,* Edited by National Seminars Publications, Shawnee Mission, Kansas, Lifestyle Series, 1989

McKay, Dawn Rosenberg, About.com, Career Planning, *Computer Literacy An Important Skill,* http://careerplanning.about.com/od/importantskills/a/com_literacy.htm, a part of The New York Times Company, 2010

McKay, Dawn Rosenberg, About.com, Career Planning, *Give Yourself the Competitive Edge, The Skills You Need To Be Competitive in Today's Workplace,* http://careerplanning.about.com/od/worksplacesurvival/a/competitive.htm, a part of The New York Times Company, 2010

McKay, Dawn Rosenberg, About.com, Career Planning, *How To Deal With the Unexpected (or Just Another Day at the Office),* http://careerplanning.about.com/od/workplacesurvival/a/unexpected.htm, a part of The New York Times Company, 2010

McKay, Dawn Rosenberg, About.com, Career Planning, *Inappropriate Dress and Conduct May Send the Wrong Message, What Do Your Clothes Say About You?,* http://careerplanning.about.com/cs/dressingforwork/a/inapprop_dress.htm, a part of The New York Times Company, 2010

McKay, Dawn Rosenberg, About.com, Career Planning, *Writing Skills, Why Writing Skills Are Important,* http://careerplanning.about.com/cs/miscskills/a/writing_skills/htm, a part of The New York Times Company, 2010

McKay, Dawn Rosenberg, About.com, Career Planning, *Questions to Ask Yourself Before You Get Dressed for a Job Interview,* http://careerplanning.about.com/od/jobinterviews/a/dress_questions.htm, a part of The New York Times Company, 2010

Nellis, Cynthia, About.com, *Women's Fashion, Top 6 Career Looks on a Budget,* http:;//fashion.about.com/od/toppicks/topbudgetcareer,htm, a part of The New York Times Company, 2010

Thomas, Marian, *A New Attitude,* Edited by National Press Publications, Shawnee Mission, Kansas, Productivity Series, 1991

Towers, Mark, *Self-Esteem: The Power to Be Your Best,* Edited by National Press Publications, Shawnee Mission, Kansas, Lifestyle Series, 1991

Tracy, Brian, *GOALS! How To Get Everything You Want Faster Than You Ever Thought Possible,* Berrett-Koehler Publishers, Inc., 2003, 2004

Wallace, Joanne, speaker and author, www.joannewallace.com.

Watson, Donna, PhD, *101 Simple Ways To Be Good To Yourself,* Energy Press, A Bard Productions Book, 1993

Watson, Donna, PhD, *Let Go and Live, How To Beat Stress & Build Self Esteem,* six-tape album, The Donna Watson Group, 1995

Yoder, Elmon E., *Power Presentation Skills*, Edited by National Press Publications, Shawnee Mission, Kansas, Communication Series, 1988

Want to Share Your Ideas?

Connect with others who are learning and growing in their careers. We would love to have you join our ever-growing circle of friends and share your best ideas for success.

www.howtogetandkeepajob.com

www.facebook.com/howtogetandkeepajob

www.twitter.com/getandkeepajob